first

season

FIRST SEASON / ISRAEL HOROVITZ

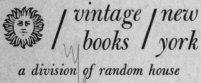

vintage / new
books / york
a division of random house

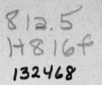

VINTAGE BOOKS EDITION, November 1968

to my children
and their friends,
with love

"Sleep with dogs,
wake with fleas."

—Webster (or someone like that)

contents /

preface   between the lines

My first New York season consisted of four plays premiered and reviewed within a period of four months. I've been writing plays for ten years. The writing of the four plays of the season spans a period of three years. But in the eyes of the ticketholder and critic, it is as though these plays appeared by magic, a mere moment after some berserk blue bulb lit over my head. So that while the ecstasy is rather evident in my first season, I'll give you a hint of some of the ashes that were tasted along the way.

And *Line* was the beginning.

Rehearsals for *Line* smacked of a sort of erotic joy. It was all too good. We were to open at the Café La Mama, which meant there were no backers or producers around with Important Concepts. There was no investment to recoup, except for Ellen Stewart's one hundred dollars, which was an out-and-out gift (one hundred one dollar bills). I had the director I wanted, the cast—and even the stage manager I preferred. Everything a skinny, frightened kid could want. I even had the joy of knowing I could keep the critics away if I so chose. A La Mama production is just that lovely.

Without the commercial pressures of Broadway, or worse yet, off-Broadway, we found we all worked harder than any of us could ever imagine. I did three hundred pages of rewrites for a play that had a running time of just over one hour and fifteen minutes. We rehearsed five weeks, instead of the normal two. We worked. It was all going so well, I was more frightened than I've ever been in my life. After all, where was the calamity?

Then, the day before we opened, the actor who had been playing the lead, the role of Stephen, got an emergency call to do something terribly important in Hollywood. He went away on a jet and never came back.

At last, the calamity!

As I packed up my wife and my pencils, happily heading home to another year of obscure, blissful tragedy, Jimmy Hammerstein, the director and Oscar's son, proposed the dumbest idea I'd ever heard: I would take a script and sit, center stage, reading the role of Stephen. What he knew and I didn't was that I knew every word of the play and would act the hell out of it on opening night.

The rest is history.

Jerry Tallmer of the *New York Post* wrote an unprecedented review headlined "WELCOME, MR. HOROVITZ" and I giggled and wept, both at the same time. That was my first review in a New York daily newspaper.

And my First Season began.

While *Line* was in rehearsal, and indeed for two years prior, my agent had been negotiating with every living, breathing producer for a production of my two plays *It's Called the Sugar Plum* and *The Indian Wants the Bronx*. Whenever a producer liked *Indian*, he hated *Sugar Plum*. Whenever a producer liked *Sugar Plum*, he hated *Indian*.

And all variations on that theme. Jules Irving, in fact, had approached us for a production of *The Indian Wants the Bronx* at Lincoln Center's Forum Theatre. Just *Indian*. He hated *Sugar Plum*.

Usually I never know what I want, only what I don't want, but in this case I didn't want another "protected" production of my plays. I'd been a playwright/member of the Eugene O'Neill Memorial Theatre Foundation since its inception and had lived through staged-readings of both plays there. This time I wanted a commercial production: I simply wanted to see if my plays could sell tickets.

Suddenly the plays were optioned, and January 17, 1968, was set as the opening date with the League of New York Theatres. Remember both plays were "old" to me. *The Indian Wants the Bronx* had gone through four productions: at the Loft Workshop in New York, the O'Neill Foundation in Connecticut, the Canoe Place Cabaret Theatre on Long Island and the Act IV Theatre in Provincetown. *It's Called the Sugar Plum* had had an excellent staged-reading at the O'Neill Foundation in July, 1967. But just as suddenly these were both new plays. And they were terribly important as new plays in my First Season.

To make matters all the more confusing, one of my personal philosophies is that I must always have a new play. It is a simple ploy: when someone rejects my old play, I can always brag about the wonders of my new play. In the case of *It's Called the Sugar Plum* and *The Indian Wants the Bronx*, my *new* play had been *Line!* But my new play had already been produced and reviewed by all the major critics before my old plays.

And that's why I wrote *Rats* during the rehearsal period for *Indian* and *Sugar Plum*. And that's also why the rehearsals of *Indian* and *Sugar Plum* represented an entirely new kind of agony. Whatever would happen to me with old plays?

We began rehearsals at Stage 73 in New York City. We were scheduled to open at the East 74th Street Playhouse, a marvelous 299-seat house. In fact, it all had been announced in the newspapers via the press agent Howard Atlee and Hammerstein had signed to direct the new plays. There was also a production of *Line* going on at the same time somewhere in Vermont. Hammerstein and I thought it would be quite brilliant to take a couple of days in ski country, see *Line*, and talk the hell out of *Indian* and *Sugar Plum*. We were planning the perfect production, of course.

En route to Vermont to see what would be, for the season, the final production that I would allow of *Line* in its one-act form, we stopped to call our producer. We asked about the contract for the girl we had cast as the lead in *Sugar Plum*. It seems that our producer had signed all the actors to some weird kind of equality contract that promised everybody they'd starve at exactly the same rate of pay. Our first choice for the role of Joanna Dibble had no intention of starving at all and was lost forever to nonequality. And further, we'd lost our theatre to a cheaper number called the Astor Place Theatre, which, as luck would have it, isn't on Astor Place.

We drove numbly on to Vermont and watched the actors run through a performance of *Line* for us alone, as nobody else showed. Jimmy called his wife, I called my wife. I'm not sure whether he was laughing or crying in the next phone booth, because I was laughing and crying too hard to hear anything at all.

Hammerstein had a brand-new car, a gorgeous foreign job, whose engine froze in the Vermont freeze and split into two incredible pieces of pop sculpture, unfortunately and obviously decorative rather than functional, so we rented a Hertz car. A local stand-up comedian directed us to New York via Montreal, and thirty hours later we arrived safely home in the jungle of New York, just in time for rehearsal.

We worked *Indian* by day and roamed the streets looking for a Joanna Dibble by night. There were immediately two problems: we had cast an unfortunate East Indian who couldn't act a credible East Indian, which makes for a hell of a mess in any play called *The Indian Wants the Bronx,* and after reading two hundred Miss Dibbles, we decided that *It's Called the Sugar Plum* had to be the world's most impossible play.

I had written *Sugar Plum* as a backward play: its highest emotional peak is reached at the beginning, with Joanna Dibble's entrance. In theory, that's just swell. In reality, we had girls collapsing during auditions, calling us nasty names, and the kind of peaceful panic that lets you know you're really getting nowhere. We finally settled on a Joanna Dibble, poor dear, and settled into the reality of the traps of that play. When *Line* doesn't quite work, it's still all right. That we saw in Vermont. When *The Indian Wants the Bronx* doesn't quite work, it falls into a kind of first-level drama that's thin, but still all right. That I had seen at the O'Neill Conference, and truthfully through the first five or six drafts of the play until I hit upon the off-stage character of Pussyface, the social worker. When *It's Called the Sugar Plum* doesn't quite work, it's deadly. Again, it's a backward play. And that's a bastard.

Quite simply, when Joanna Dibble's entrance isn't totally believable, when the audience is *asked* to *accept* the premise of the play, it just doesn't happen. Sometimes in rehearsals it happened. Once it happened so well I was terrified by my own decision to call the evening *The Indian Wants the Bronx.* On that day, *Sugar Plum* looked terrific and *Indian* had the Indian who couldn't act Indian.

We rehearsed and rehearsed and rehearsed. At that time I was writing and directing television commercials full time for an advertising agency. I was a sure candidate for the sack at work, because I never worked on any proper time schedule. In truth, the owners of the agency are close personal friends, but my fantasies never spell simple trouble, always total disaster. And of course the plays didn't look like anything *I'd* pay money to see, so it was for the moment all agony. Pure, but all agony.

We transferred our pathetic little group from the Stage 73 rehearsal hall to the Astor Place Theatre to set up and work on stage and ready ourselves for previews. Unfortunately, the scenery had been designed for the East 74th Street Playhouse, and didn't begin to fit on the tiny stage at Astor Place. Also, the entire directorial concept had been set for the other theatre and had to be readjusted for a theatre without wings for entrances and exits. Both plays have a couple of those. Most unfortunate, my cab driver didn't know where the hell the Astor Place Theatre was. And neither did I.

The set was redesigned and constructed. The direction changed fiercely to keep the actors out of the way of the furniture. And previews began.

The Indian Wants the Bronx was so bad, *It's Called the Sugar Plum* looked just fine. We were in trouble.

John Cazale is a wonderful actor who had played Gupta, the Indian, the previous summer in Provincetown. True, John's Italian, not Hindu. True, John's from Winchester, Massachusetts, not Delhi. But it's also true that John Cazale is a fine, sensitive actor. Happily, Cazale had played Dolan in *Line* at La Mama, so not only had Jimmy directed him before, but Ruth Newton, the producer, had seen him act. Even better, Al Pacino, the brilliant young actor who played Murph and who was ultimately a great force in the success of this production of *The Indian Wants the Bronx*, had worked in the same play with Cazale that summer in Provincetown. So we proceeded to enter the most painful situation a director and playwright can be in: we fired an actor and replaced him with Cazale—just before opening.

Suddenly, *Indian* came to life. Every nuance I had dreamed of was available. The actors changed from hired players to a marvelous kind of ensemble. We transcended the play and became a Theatre. The rest is history as well. There are always two levels of reality that never join: the writing of plays and the success of plays. We got lucky, because *The Indian Wants the Bronx* got the finest reviews of any play in New York during the 1967–68 season.

It's Called the Sugar Plum missed. I'll take the blame. If a play has traps, it has flaws, and the traps and the flaws were evident on opening night. It wasn't ready. Some of the critics saw through the production and liked the play. Some of the critics did the most biting thing a critic can do: they ignored the play. In any case the play lives and will be done again—London, Bucharest, East Berlin, Spoleto, plus American regional theatres and college theatres. There are productions planned and some of them are bound to succeed with *Sugar Plum*. New York, in this country, is only the beginning for a play.

Rats came next. I had somehow managed to get through a draft of *Rats* during the rehearsal and preview period of *The Indian Wants the Bronx*. *Rats* is a gruesome play about two rats and a baby in a crib in Harlem. Although I have a paranoiac philosophy that drives me to always have a new play in the works while an old play is being done, I've never and will never write a play unless I'm compelled by the subject of that play. Even with the knowledge that many people would be and are repulsed by the first-level violence of *The Indian Wants the Bronx*, I had to write *Rats*. There is little any of us can do to change the world. God knows a little play isn't the answer, but it's the best I can do.

Obviously *Rats* was written before the assassination of

Dr. Martin Luther King; obviously *Rats* was written before the summer of 1968; obviously *Rats* was written before the presidential election of 1968; obviously *Rats* was written during the Vietnam War. Again, it's the best—perhaps better said, the most—I can do.

Rehearsals for *Rats* were strange. My First Season was well underway when they began. Even though just four months had passed since the opening of *Line,* my name had appeared in almost every newspaper and magazine in the country. The *Village Voice* had run a three-page article entitled "Will Success Spoil Israel Horovitz?" The *New York Times* had called *The Indian Wants the Bronx* "one of the most hopeful things in the New York Theatre." The *New York Post* had run a feature article about me called "Young Man in a Hurry." Everybody Big had called me by then: the Hollywood people, the Important New York producers. It had happened.

Rats was done on a program of eleven playlets in one evening called *Collision Course.* It was directed by Edward Parone and opened at Café Au Go Go, and subsequently moved to the Actors' Playhouse on 7th Avenue. Because there were eleven plays involved, I couldn't thrust myself into rehearsals and intimidate everybody as I had with my other plays earlier in the year. And although— because of the production—few people realized the rats were rats until the end of the play, the reviews were glowing. Lots to giggle about. Lots to brag about. Lots. But because *Rats* was the last play of my First Season, the end of my First Season, it was a time for reflection. Until then there had been little time to think. Little time to rest. Little time.

The Void.

Before my First Season there was a void. A void I thought was invisibility itself. Suddenly there was a clamor to read my next play. Lots of ugly people got friendly. Worst of all, some of my dearest friends got ugly.

Line is now incredibly important to me, not because it's to be done on Broadway in its new full-length form, but for a far greater reason. I mentioned the traps in *It's Called the Sugar Plum. Line* doesn't have those traps, but it is more than a play, it's an environment. And this is the New Theatre.

In the supposed good old days, Eugene O'Neill could hand his script over to a director and separate himself from the unclean theatre to be with his real people. Eugene O'Neill would fail today. Today's theatre is environment. A play is a bore; the new theatre is surprise. And that requires a new kind of involvement. I don't think a playwright can afford to break from substance for form. That's fraudulent. But once the substance, the thing that troubles the playwright enough to write a play, is settled, it will dictate a form. And in our theatre today there are no rules of form. We're writing them now, perhaps. There has been too much emphasis on the star playwright, the star actor, the star director, the star (forgive me) producer. It's hardly a vision of genius to note these damned stars are killing us. We desperately need star theatres, where good actors and good directors work conscientiously on good plays until a kind of total environment springs to life.

That happened when we did *Line.* I didn't invite an audience to see my play, I invited an audience into my world. One of the New York newspapers called *Line* "a crazy thing," and that's terribly accurate. But what emotion goes sailing through that crazy thing! How marvelous to laugh and cry during the same play. The key to it all seems to be the production. Once there were good plays and good productions or one or the other. Today, if the media is the massage, then the production is in fact the play. The play with traps traps itself. The environmental play lends itself to free production and can succeed. This is an enormous change. For now the playwright must extend himself and be able to act, or certainly know how actors do their stuff. He must be able to direct. In short, he should know how a play is produced and publicized and put on. Playwrights are not trapped into the electronic age, we're reveling in it. But we must write for it as well. Today a playwright must be capable of creating an event from his play as a part of a theatre-in-motion. And this theatre-in-motion is in fact created from the play itself, as a base. But once the baby breathes life, the father must be capable of sheltering and feeding the child as well. This may sound new, but is it?

Shakespeare produced his own plays in his own touring company. He even wrote the advertising handbills—and they were pretty good. And the Brecht Ensemble was Brecht's vision and ultimate monument beyond his plays. And Artaud toyed with and created the Theatre of Cruelty; he didn't just write a couple of cruel plays.

The list is long enough and old enough to prove that the new theatre in America is not new at all. What I discovered when I discovered just how terribly involved I was with *Line* was that I had returned to something quite ancient: the playwright out of his dumb category, jumping around all over the place and having a hell of a lot of fun. Now that's terrific!

How lovely to live *after* the Theatre of Boredom. We're free. The movies aren't killing us nor are movies better than ever. They're just movies. Film is run by electricity, so of course film is the darling of the electronic babies. But we don't have to plug in our plays. The form has been so rigid you just have to jiggle it two inches to the left and mountains move.

Back to *Line:* it is a play about people grappling for position in line. The location and description of the line is never defined. The play has no scenery, no real time sequence, no need to track the nitty-gritties of real people, for the people in the line *must* be caricatures of what people are. So, working from the substance of the play—a rather symbolic line created and ultimately destroyed by a young man dying to die younger than Mozart—all hell breaks loose in terms of form. Yet the play falls delightfully into a category previously held by situation comedies: the line, abstract as it may seem, is the situation. The horror is the comedy. But I can barely take credit for much of *Line*'s success. Because the theatre was going into a new climate, because the theatre was willing to stand for the many plays this season as good as *Line*, there was finally a chance for some fun.

It is, simply, fun to be involved with theatre that can be truly social, political, psychological. It is, simply, fun to experience a production in which the audience becomes a part of the production by virtue of actors talking directly into the house, or walking into the house, or sitting in the house, or any of the supposed crazy things we can do now.

And as an undercurrent to the whole wonderful season was the off-Broadway–off-off-Broadway conflict. I am plagued, as are most serious playwrights and playgoers, by the contest off-Broadway and off-off-Broadway as to who can be the most bizarre. Again, form for its own sake is ultimately childish and more often boring than not. Although the most bizarre and boring plays seem to show themselves in the café theatres and off-off-Broadway houses more than the off-Broadway houses, this is quite simply homage to the fact that off-Broadway is now an extension of Broadway, artistically and economically, and this entire limbo area of theatre called off-Broadway is in fact dead, with little or no reason for being. This is a healthy sign, not at all frightening. The distinction between what off-Broadway should do and what off-off-Broadway actually does is enormous only in terms of what things cost, productions and tickets alike. The void that off-Broadway filled twenty years ago *had* to give way in the past few years, or, inversely, had to return to what was, and of course why it all happened in the first place. Because the unions and the critics and the lovely spirit of amateurism in the absolute had decidedly been snatched away from off-Broadway, off-off-Broadway *had* to fill the void. The only pity of it all is the unfortunate name for the new area, off-off-Broadway. It sounds ridiculous. Happily, at best and quite frequently, off-off-Broadway theatre displays the seriousness and lovely spirit one expects from amateur theatre.

But inevitably as the door opens for young writers and the chance to be seen quickly, easily and earnestly is given us, this very gift is abused and the results are most often bizarre and ill-conceived. But in spite of this there is order. Writers who are bizarre for the sake of being bizarre seem to disappear and the more serious writers, off-off-Broadway, have actually made valid reputations throughout the world theatre as quickly and easily and earnestly as their plays were seen.

Ellen Stewart's tour with her La Mama Troupe throughout Europe was a total success. The plays that toured were good and every playwright represented was certainly deadly serious. The tour brought the first smack of respectability to off-off-Broadway, long before some of these plays were even seen in this country. I don't think anyone has ever discussed the tour in this light, but I do think that this was Miss Stewart's primary goal, and thus her success. But of course there's always a flaw, if not a calamity. With newfound respectability in a country of superstars, La Mama suddenly faces the burden of becoming an Important Proving-ground for Young Talent. This had not yet happened in November-December, 1967, at the time of my production of *Line*, but it was starting. Now the critics are there nightly. Now it's the place to be seen, not just on stage, but in the audience as well. I hope, selfishly I suppose, that Café La Mama isn't spoiled completely by good intention. I am fond enough of Ellen Stewart to fear for her and I know that the failure of success would crush her vision.

What happened during my First Season was certainly a turning point, but not only for me; it was a year of change. My First Season arrived and with it the two realities of writing plays and plays succeeding. Although these realities never join, somehow they did. And that's incredible luck.

But this is still the theatre that makes a First Season like mine add up to nothing more or less than the horrifyingly obvious: a chance for a Second Season.

Israel Horovitz
Spring, 1968

first

season

line /

Line: Israel Horovitz as STEPHEN and John Cazale (winner of the 1968 OBIE Award for Distinguished Performance in *Line*) as DOLAN.

LINE, *in a one-act version, was presented by Ellen Stewart on November 29, 1967, at Café LaMama ETC, New York City, with the following cast:*

(*In order of appearance*)

FLEMING   Paul Haller
STEPHEN   Israel Horovitz
MOLLY   Ann Wedgeworth
DOLAN   John Cazale
ARNALL   Michael Del Medico

Directed by   James Hammerstein
Assistant Director   Bonnie Frindel

Setting: A line.

Time: The present.

*The stage is without scenery.
A fat line of white tape is on the floor, to the extreme stage
right.* FLEMING, *a "war-vet," stands waiting at the line . . .
waiting . . . waiting.*

FLEMING *is in his late thirties; balding, paunchy, vulgar
at a glance. He is pinspotted in a pool of light that indicates
the moment when late night turns to early morning. He is
waiting . . . waiting. His feet are planted solidly at the
line, rigid, yet his body bends with exhaustion. He is waiting . . . waiting.*

*He dips into a sack and produces a bag of potato chips, a
can of beer (flip-top) and a cloth napkin. He tucks the
napkin into his shirt top, opens the beer, eats the chips,
drinks, belches and does it all again. He never moves his
feet from the mark.*

FLEMING (*Singing*)
  Take me out to the ball game,
  Take me out to the park,
  Buy me some peanuts and what's his name . . .
  I don't care if you never what do you call it.
    (*Louder now*)
  Take me out to the ball game,
  Buy me lots of your stuff . . .
  Dumm diddy dumm-dumm di dummm di dumm.
  That's where I want to be.
    (*He drinks again and belches*)
  Buy me some peanuts and what's his jacks,
  I don't care if I never get back . . .

9

And will root, root, root for the home thing . . .
Root 'til our voices run dry,
If you'll take me out to the ball game,
I'll never want to go home.

> (STEPHEN *enters and sits down, facing away from* FLEMING. *He has entered quietly, neither noticing* FLEMING, *nor has he been noticed by* FLEMING. STEPHEN *is carrying a letter. He has been weeping, his face tearstained. He hears* FLEMING)

FLEMING (*Singing*)
Take me out to the park,
Buy me some peanuts and crackerthings . . .
Dumm di dumm dumm di dumm dumm dumm dumm.
> (STEPHEN *makes a decision to play a game. He straightens up and walks to* FLEMING. *As soon as* STEPHEN *is up,* FLEMING *notices him and stops singing, awaiting to hear what* STEPHEN *will say*)

STEPHEN   Is this the line? (FLEMING *stares* STEPHEN *in the eye, but does not answer*) Excuse me, mister. Is this a line? (FLEMING *turns his back on* STEPHEN, *after carefully studying* STEPHEN's *manner and clothing and age*) Is this a line, huh?

FLEMING (*After a long take*)   What's it look like?

STEPHEN (*Spots the tape on the floor*)   Oh, yeah. There it is. It's a line all right. It's a beautiful line. (*He caresses the tape, then straightens and faces* FLEMING) *I couldn't* tell from back there. I would have been earlier if I had started out earlier. You wouldn't think anyone would be damn fool enough to get up this early. Or not go to bed. Depending on how you look at it. (FLEMING *stares at* STEPHEN *incredulously*) Oh, I didn't mean you were a damn fool. (*Pauses*) Not yet. Nice line. Just the two of us, huh?

FLEMING What's it look like? What's it look like?

STEPHEN That's all you ever say, huh? "What's it look like?"—"What's it look like?" (*Pauses*) Must be nice.

FLEMING Huh?

STEPHEN Being first. Right up front of the line like that. Singing away. Singing your damn fool heart out. I could hear you from back there. Singing your damn fool heart out. You like music? (FLEMING *turns his back to* STEPHEN, *who now begins to talk with incredible speed*) I'm a music nut myself. Mozart. He's the one. I've got all his records. Started out on seventy-eight. Then I moved on to thirty-three and a third when I got to be thirteen or so. Now I've got him on hi-fi, stereo and transistorized snap-in cartridges. (*Displays his portable tape recorder*) I've got him on everything he's on. (*Pauses*) Must be nice. (*Pauses*) Want to trade places?

FLEMING You yak like that all the time?

STEPHEN (*Peeks over* FLEMING'S *shoulder at the LINE*) That's a good solid line. I've seen some skimpy little lines, but that one's a beauty. (*Whistles a strain from* "The Magic Flute") That's Mozart. Want me to whistle some more? Or we could sing your song. "Take Me Out to the Ball Game." I know most of the pop songs from your twenties, your thirties and your forties. I'm bad on your fifties and your sixties. That's when *I* started composing. And, of course, that's when Mozart really started getting in the way. But, have it like you will—just name the

tune. 'Course, don't get me wrong. I'd rather be whis-
tling my own songs any day of the week. Any night, for
that matter. Or whistle Mozart. "The Magic Flute."
"Marriage of Figaro." Go on. Just "Name That Tune." I
can sing it in Italian, German, French, or your English.
Hell, if he could knock them out at seven, I should be
able to whistle at thirty, right? Christ, I am thirty, too.
Not thirty-two. Thirty *also*. Three-o. Thirty. He was
thirty-five. Around the age of Christ. What hath God
wrought? God hath wrought iron! (*Pauses. Waits to see
if* FLEMING *has crumbled yet. Sees* FLEMING'S *confused,
but still on his feet, so* STEPHEN *continues*) Thirty-five.
That's how old he was. He thought he was writing his
funeral music all right. He was, too. Isn't that something,
to have that kind of premonition? That's what you call
your young genius. The only real genius ever to walk on
this earth, mister. Wolfgang Amadeus Mozart. W-A-M.
(*Yells right into* FLEMING'S *face*) WAM! WAM! WAM!
(FLEMING, *thunderstruck, turns and overtly snubs* STE-
PHEN. STEPHEN *takes his wallet out of his pocket and
studies its contents carefully. Then he pokes* FLEMING,
who turns about menacingly)

STEPHEN You want to read my wallet?

FLEMING Huh?

STEPHEN (*Begins to unfold an enormous credit-card case*)
You want to read my wallet? You can read my wallet and
I'll read your wallet. You can learn a lot about people
from their wallets. Avis cards. Hertz cards. American
Express. Air Travel. Bloomingdale's. Sak's. Old phone
numbers. Bits and scraps. Contraceptives. Locks of hair.
Baby pictures. Calendars. Business cards from insurance
men, advertising men, gasoline-station men, newspaper-

men, thin men, fat men, good men, bad men, brilliant men, sneaky men, and the ladies. Businessladies have cards. ID cards. Not the ladies, I mean. I mean the men who own the wallets who you're learning about, right?

FLEMING (*Sings*)
Take me out to the ball game,
Take me out to the park.

STEPHEN Hey. Don't turn your back on me, huh? Let me read your wallet. I've read mine before. I read my wallet all the time. Hey, will you? Here. Take my wallet, then. You don't even have to let me read yours. (*Forces his wallet into* FLEMING's *hands.* FLEMING *is absolutely astonished*) That's it. Go on. Read. (FLEMING *obeys, wide-eyed*) There. See that ID card? That lets you know who I am, right away. See? Stephen. Steve. Or Stevie. And where I work. See that? Now look at the pictures. My kids. That one's dead. That one's dead. That one's dead. That one's dead. There are more. Don't stop. More pictures.

> (STEPHEN *leaves the wallet in* FLEMING's *hand and begins a wide circle around him, almost forcing* FLEMING *out of line*)

FLEMING How'd you lose all those kids?

STEPHEN Lose the kids?

FLEMING Dead. All these dead kids? (*Sees that the pictures are lithographs of Mozart*) Hey! Those are drawings!

STEPHEN Who said they were kids?

FLEMING (*Waits, staring*) Oh, boy. Here we go. (*Sings, after jamming* STEPHEN's *wallet back into* STEPHEN's *pocket*)

> Take me out to the ball game,
> Take me out to the park,
> Buy me some peanuts and crackerthings . . .
> (STEPHEN *joins in. In unison*)
> We don't care if we never get back.
> (FLEMING *stops*)

STEPHEN

> For it's a root, root, root for the home . . .
> (*Stops. Asks*)

Do you really think this line is for the ball game? Huh? There's no ball game around here. I mean, I wouldn't be here if there was a ball game. Ball games aren't my kind of stuff. I loathe ball games, myself. You like ball games?

FLEMING (*At this point, the situation has gone beyond* FLEMING's *comprehension, and his confusion is obvious*) Who are you?

STEPHEN That's why I gave you my wallet. If everybody would just pass their wallets around, sooner or later something would happen, right?

FLEMING Yeah.

STEPHEN Can you imagine if you met the President and he gave you his wallet to read? You'd know everything about him. Or the Mayor. Kings. Ballplayers, even. Read THEIR wallets. Boy, would you know it all soon enough. Scraps of paper that held secrets they forgot were secrets. Meetings they were supposed to make. Locks of hair. Pictures of babies they forgot they had. Names.

Addresses. ID cards. Secret money hidden in secret places. Hertz cards. Avis cards. Air Travel cards. You'd know everything, wouldn't you? (STEPHEN *has* FLEMING *going now. He increases the speed of his delivery, eyes flickering, hands waving, watching* FLEMING's *terrified responses*) You see, friend, all those up-front people are fakes. Fakes. There's never been a real first place . . . never a real leader. Except you know who. War heroes? All frauds. If there had been one really efficient war, we wouldn't be here, would we?

FLEMING   I'm first. All I know is, I'm first.

STEPHEN   First. It's just a word. Twist the letters around, you get strif. God backwards. Dog. Split the first three letters off of therapist, you get two words: the rapist. Spell Hannah backwards, you get Hannah. Spell backwards backwards, you get sdrawkcab. I tell you, show me one of your so-called winners, and let me have one look at his wallet; just one. I'll never have to count the money, either. There's never been a real first before. Never. I know, friend. I know. See that line? Turn it on end, you know what you've got? A number one. But how do you hang on to it? How do you really hold it, so you're not one of those wallet-carrying, secret-compartment fakes like all of them? Answer that question and I'd let you follow me in. You could be second.

FLEMING   What do you mean "second"? I'm first. I'm right at the front.

STEPHEN   For the moment.

FLEMING   Don't get any smart ideas.

STEPHEN   The only conclusions I draw are on men's-room walls. Now if you'd shut up for a while, I'll sing my wallet. (FLEMING *takes his beer and does some serious drinking.* STEPHEN *sings*) This nontransferable Hertz charge card entitles the person named to use Hertz Rent-A-Car service under the terms of the Hertz Rental Agreement on a credit basis. Where you desire to make immediate payments, the card enables you to rent without deposit. Payment for rentals charged is due within ten days after the billing date. (*As* STEPHEN *continues,* MOLLY, *a thirtyish, plump woman wanders on the stage and stares quizzically at* STEPHEN *and* FLEMING) This card is subject to invalidation and modification without notice and is the property of the Hertz system . . . (STEPHEN *notices* MOLLY) Hey. You looking for the line, lady?

MOLLY   Line?

STEPHEN   That's right. This is a line. You're third. Number three. There used to be just two of us here. Me and Fleming. This is Fleming. Who are you?

FLEMING   How'd you know my name, huh? How'd you know my name?

STEPHEN   (*To* FLEMING) I read your wallet. (*To* MOLLY) You're third. That's not too bad. You won't have to wait long.

FLEMING   (*Checks to see if* STEPHEN *has stolen his wallet, then screams*) You didn't read my wallet! Nobody's read my wallet, except me!

MOLLY   (*Joining the line*) Third? I'm third, huh? How long have you been waiting?

STEPHEN   About ten minutes. Fleming must have been here all night. Were you here all night, Fleming? He looks it, huh?

FLEMING   How the hell did you know my name? How'd you know?

MOLLY   Third place. How soon do they open?

STEPHEN   You'll probably see a crowd before that. There's always a crowd. The people who say, "Maybe there won't be a crowd, let's go anyway." Those people. You'll see them. Won't she, Fleming?

FLEMING   How'd you know my name? How'd you know my name?

STEPHEN   Fleming, don't be a bore! What's your name? Mine's Stephen.

MOLLY   Molly. I'm Molly.

STEPHEN   Hello, Molly. Glad you're third. Fleming, this is Molly.

MOLLY   Hello.

FLEMING   Hey, kid. Hold our places in line. Come here, m'am. (*Takes her aside, whispers*) That kid's crazy. Watch out. He's one of them weirdos. He's been saying crazy things to me.

STEPHEN   (*Moves into first position*)   I can't guarantee your places. The crowd's going to come sure as hell and I can't guarantee anybody's place. The fact is, Fleming, I'm first now.

17

FLEMING What?

STEPHEN I'm first. (*Straddles the line*) Look at me. I'm up first. Up front. Front of the line.
(MOLLY *jumps into second position*)

MOLLY You could have held our places. Nobody else is here.

STEPHEN It's just not right. Besides, Fleming wouldn't hold anybody's place. You can tell that just from looking at him. He's never held anybody's place in his life.

FLEMING (*Enraged, but trying to maintain control*) Kid, I've been standing there all night. All night. Waiting. Waiting in the front of the line. The very front. Now I think you'd better let me get right back up there. (*As* FLEMING *continues,* DOLAN *enters and walks toward the line*) Just step back one pace and let me in there. (DOLAN *quietly steps into line behind* MOLLY. DOLAN *is* FLEMING'S *age, as strong. To* DOLAN) I'm up front.

DOLAN Huh?

FLEMING I'm first. That kid just took my spot. You're fourth.

DOLAN I don't mean to argue, but I count third. You're fourth.

FLEMING Hey. Listen. That kid grabbed my place. I waited all night up front. Right at the front of the line.

DOLAN I don't want to argue, but you're not getting in front of me, pal, so skip it.

FLEMING Skip it? Bull, I'll skip it. (*Walks up to* STEPHEN) Give me back my place, kid, or I'll knock you out of it. (STEPHEN *drops to the floor and curls up into a ball.* FLEMING *stares, again astonished*) Get up!

DOLAN I hate to argue, but get out of the front, mac! The kid was up front and I'm third. The lady's second.

MOLLY He *was* up front, actually.

DOLAN Well, he can go second if you want him to, lady. I'm third.
(ARNALL *enters and walks directly into the line*)

ARNALL Molly?

MOLLY Arnall. Here I am.

ARNALL You think I can't see you? You saved my place?

MOLLY (*To* DOLAN) I was saving his place, sir. We had an arrangement.

DOLAN Not that I want to run things, but that's too bad. No place was saved. He can go fourth.

FLEMING I'm fourth! For Christ's sake what am I saying? I'm *first*.

ARNALL (*Jumps into fourth position*) I'm fourth.

MOLLY I'm second.

DOLAN I'm third.

STEPHEN (*After the stampede, to* DOLAN) Obviously, I'm first. My name's Stephen. Who are you?

DOLAN Dolan's what they call me. How long you been waiting?

STEPHEN About twelve and a half minutes.

ARNALL Jesus. If I could have found my clean shirts, Molly . . . If I could have found where you hid them . . . I would have been here half an hour ago. I would have been first.

FLEMING I've been here all night.

ARNALL How come you're fifth? (*Pause for a "take" from* FLEMING) You're not even in line. Why aren't you first?

FLEMING I *am* first, God damn it! I *am* first. That crazy kid grabbed my place. How'd you know my name, kid?

ARNALL Fleming?

FLEMING How the hell do *you* know?

ARNALL (*Pulls* FLEMING'S *T-shirt-neck to his eyes*) It's written on your undershirt.
(FLEMING *spins around trying to read the label*)

STEPHEN I read your undershirt.

FLEMING (*To* DOLAN) Look, I've been here all night. I've been standing right at the front of the line all night. You know that's true. (*To* MOLLY) You saw me here, lady. You know I was first.

MOLLY You stepped out of line. (*To* ARNALL) He stepped out of line, Arnall.

ARNALL Serves you right, then, Fleming. If I could have found my clean shirt, I would have been first. My dumb wife hides my dumb shirts. Isn't that terrific? She hides my shirts. I could have been first by half an hour. But she hid my shirt. You know where I found it? (*Simply*) I couldn't find it.

STEPHEN (*Passes chewing gum to everyone but* FLEMING) Want some Wrigley's spearmint chewing gum?

ALL Thanks . . . thanks . . . thank you.
(*Ad libs as they unwrap their gum and begin to chew. Everyone stops talking and does some serious gum-chewing for a full minute while* FLEMING *paces up and down the line, furious, but contained*)

FLEMING This is ridiculous. I was first. All night. (*To* ARNALL) I just took your wife aside to warn her about that crazy kid. He jumped the line. He jumped in front. That's not fair, is it? I was here all night.

DOLAN You're fifth. There's plenty here for five. You'll get your chance.

FLEMING (*To* ARNALL) That's not the point, God damn it. There's only one first and I waited up all night. All night in the line all by myself. And he took it away from me. Now that is definitely unfair.

ARNALL (*Completely against* FLEMING's *problem*) I hate to go anywhere at night with the shirt from the day still on. You never know what kind of germs you come in contact with during the day. You never can tell, can you?

STEPHEN   Life's full of dirt.

ARNALL   Our place is full of dirt. My wife never cleans. If it were up to her, we'd be up to our necks in dirt. Day and night. That's why I'm late. What movie's playing?

FLEMING   Movie?

ARNALL   I thought we were going to the movies, Molly?

MOLLY   Arnall, don't cause a scene!

STEPHEN   Your shirt looks very clean to me, Arnall.

ARNALL   Looks are deceptive. Hospitals look clean, don't they? But if you ever ran a check for germcount, oh boy, wouldn't you get a score? After all, people come there— to hospitals—because they're ridden with germs. Take an old building full of germridden people, paint it stark white, you got yourself a place that looks clean, but underneath that look, there's a mess going on.

STEPHEN   How do you feel about that, Fleming? Do germ-counts disturb you too?

FLEMING   Don't get smart with me, kid. I was waiting here a long time before you, and you know it. (*To* DOLAN) He's trying to distract your attention from the fact that he *took* first place . . . he didn't earn it. No, sir. *I* earned it. I waited up for first place. He took it!

DOLAN   Well, I don't want to be the one who starts any arguments, but he *is* in first place, and he was in first place when I first got here.

STEPHEN   Fair *is* fair, Fleming!

FLEMING (*Yells*) Don't "fair" me, kid, or you'll have a fat lip to worry about!

DOLAN Now listen to me, Fleming.

FLEMING (*Screams*) What do *you* want?

DOLAN (*Screams back at him*) Lower your voice!

ARNALL Easy, Dolan, easy.

DOLAN (*To* FLEMING) Look, I don't want to start any trouble, but it seems to me if you want to be first, be first. Move the kid. If you want to be second, be second. Move his old lady. (*To* ARNALL) And don't you "easy" me. I'm nice and easy all the time. I'm Mister Niceguy. Get it? Mister Niceguy.

ARNALL Move *who*?

DOLAN Your old lady.

FLEMING Your old lady.

ARNALL You can't do that.

DOLAN And why not?

FLEMING And "why not" is right.

ARNALL She's second. She's in line. That's the way things are. She's in second place. She can beat you there.

FLEMING Hell, she did! I spent the night in first. Right up there at the white line. Got my sack here with food and drink. I'm prepared. Prepared to be first, God damn it!

23

Not second. Not third. Not fifth. I'm prepared for first. But, mind you, if I want to move your old lady and be second, I'll just move your old lady and be second. Just like that.

> ARNALL *steps out of line into* FLEMING's *way, as* FLEMING *pretends to move toward* MOLLY. FLEMING *quickly jumps into line in* ARNALL's *spot.* FLEMING *is now fourth*)

ARNALL   Hey. Hey, you dirty sonofabitch. Sonofabitch. You took my place. He took my place. What the hell is this? Get out of line, Fleming. Move out, Fleming. You took my place!

FLEMING (*Laughing*)   That's what a woman does to you, what'syourname. That's what a woman does.

ARNALL   Stop laughing, you sonofabitch!

FLEMING   That's what a woman does to you.

ARNALL (*Walks up to* MOLLY, *squares off*)   He's right! (*He slaps* MOLLY *across the face*)

MOLLY   Arnall. Arnall. Damn you. How could you? (*She chases him, slapping air around his head.* DOLAN *and* FLEMING *quickly move up one space, laughing*)

DOLAN   I'm second. I'm second.

FLEMING   I'm right behind you.

ARNALL (MOLLY *is still swatting at him*)   Now look, you bitch. Now look. We're both out. They moved up. You moved up, you sons of bitches. You snuck up.

24

DOLAN You stepped out.

STEPHEN (*Whispers*) Out of line, out of luck!

FLEMING Out of line, out of luck.

ARNALL Out of line, out of luck? That supposed to be funny, huh? That's supposed to be a joke?

FLEMING That's what a woman does to you, Arnall. You lose your place.

MOLLY You made me do that, Arnall. You made me do that.

ARNALL Shut up, you bitch. You start first with the shirts, now my place, now your place. Just shut up . . . I've got to think.

STEPHEN I'm first.

FLEMING Hey, he's not asleep.

STEPHEN When you're first you can be anything.

FLEMING Don't be smart, kid. I don't forget easily. You'll get yours.

STEPHEN
  I got mine. I'm first! (*Sings*)
    Se vuol venire nella mia scuola,
    La capriolo le insegnerò.
    Sapro ma piano—meglio ogni arcano
    Dissimulando scoprir potrò.
    L' arte schermendo, l' arte adoprando,

25

Di quà pugnando, di là scherzando,
Tuttu le macchine rovescero.
That's a song my mother taught me. I'll never forget it,
either. (*Sings*)
Se vuol venire . . .

FLEMING   Forget it. Okay?

MOLLY (*Siding up to* STEPHEN)   Your mother?
(*She kneels beside him*)

ARNALL   Stay away from him, Molly.

MOLLY   Shut your dumb mouth, Arnall. Just shut up. (*To*
STEPHEN) Is she young?

STEPHEN   "*Metza-Metz.*" (*They are both lying on the
floor. He sings*)
Se vuol venire nella mia . . .

MOLLY (*Interrupts*)   You've got a pretty face, you know
that?

ARNALL   Molly! For Christ's sake!

MOLLY (*To* STEPHEN)   Don't pay any attention to him.
(ARNALL *walks to the other side of the stage and
sits*)

STEPHEN   I'll pay attention to whom I choose. To *who* I
choose? Whatever I choose. You know what I mean.

MOLLY   I was saying that you have a pretty face.

STEPHEN   Yes, you were.

26

MOLLY Good bones. Strong bones in your face. Like James Dean.

STEPHEN James Dean?

MOLLY The movie star. The one who got killed in his Porsche. That's who you look like. James Dean.

FLEMING Who's James Dean? A movie star?

DOLAN Killed in what?

STEPHEN Is James Dean still dead?

MOLLY Don't make jokes about James Dean. He was a beautiful boy. And I'm telling you that you remind me of him.

STEPHEN I wasn't trying to be funny.

MOLLY I always wanted to make love with James Dean.

FLEMING Holy Jesus!

DOLAN Shut up.
    (*He wants to hear*)

STEPHEN Why didn't you?

MOLLY I never met him, silly. He's a movie star. And then he got killed. If I could have met him, I would have made love to him. I could have made him happy. (*Pauses*) I could make you happy.

STEPHEN I don't have a Porsche.

MOLLY (*Unfastening her blouse*) It's very warm here, don't you think? Don't you think it's very warm here?

STEPHEN (*Unbuttoning his shirt*) Yeah. I can't remember a time this hot. It makes you want to take all your clothes off, doesn't it?

MOLLY All your clothes.

STEPHEN Unbearable.
   (*He throws his shirt on the ground*)

MOLLY Unbearable. (*Throws her blouse on the ground*) Torture.
   (*She walks to* STEPHEN *and presses her body against his. They are squashed together with their hands against their stomachs, pressed together so firmly that the audience can not any longer see their hands, but can imagine what's transpiring. They sway back and forth together in a dance*)

STEPHEN (*Sings. Optional: he sings in German, French, Italian or English*)
   Should he, for instance, wish to go dancing,
   He'll face the music, I'll lead the band, yes.
   I'll lead the band.
   And then I'll take my cue, without ado,
   And slyly, very, very, very, very, very slyly.
   Using discretion, I shall uncover his secret plan.
   Subtly outwitting, innocent seeming,
   Cleverly hitting, planning and scheming,
   I'll get the best of the hypocrite yet,
   I'll beat him yet!
      (*As* STEPHEN *sings,* DOLAN *and* FLEMING *talk.* ARNALL *walks forward quietly to watch* MOLLY *and* STEPHEN

28

as they dance. STEPHEN's *song is frequently broken as he and* MOLLY *kiss fantastic kisses*)

FLEMING (*Almost a whisper*)   You've got to hand it to that kid.

DOLAN   Shh. Her old man's watching.

FLEMING   It's disgusting.

DOLAN (*Watching the lovers*)   What's disgusting?

FLEMING   Her old man's watching like that. It ain't natural.

DOLAN   Yeah. It certainly ain't natural.

FLEMING   Sonofabitch. You've got to hand it to that kid. I never would have guessed.

DOLAN   I had a woman once in a car.

FLEMING   What happened?

DOLAN   The usual thing.

FLEMING   That's all?

DOLAN   Yeah.

FLEMING   Oh.

DOLAN   I've never had a woman in a line.

FLEMING   Me neither.

DOLAN   It's funny watching like this, ain't it?

FLEMING   Yeah.

DOLAN   I'd rather be doing it.

FLEMING   Yeah.
        (*They both continue to stare goggle-eyed*)

DOLAN   I'm getting horny.

FLEMING   Yeah.

ARNALL   Yeah.
        (*Creeping his word in at their tonal level, un-
        noticed*)

FLEMING   Yeah.

DOLAN   Yeah.

ARNALL   Yeah. Yeah.

DOLAN   Yeah. Yeah.
        (*The "yeah's" start to build in a crescendo as the
        lovers reach their first climax*)

ARNALL   Yeah. Yeah.

DOLAN   Yeah. Yeah.

FLEMING   Yeah. Yeah. Yeah.

ALL   Yeah. Yeah. Yeah. Yeah. Yeah. YEAH! *YEAH!*

STEPHEN (*Sings wearily*)
　　I'll beat him yet, I'll beat him yet!
　　　　(*After they dance,* MOLLY *takes first!* STEPHEN
　　　　"*dances her*" *out of first place, tired, but not to be
　　　　undone. As he continues the song, he and* MOLLY
　　　　begin to sway again)

FLEMING　He's doing it again!

DOLAN　I can't take much more of this!

FLEMING　What are we going to do?

DOLAN　You figure it out, pal. I know what I want.
　　　　(*He jumps forward and grabs* MOLLY. *They tumble
　　　　to the side.* ARNALL *tries to jump into first position,
　　　　but* STEPHEN *punches him in the stomach and forces
　　　　him into the slot* DOLAN *vacated: second.* FLEMING
　　　　is stunned)

STEPHEN　I'm still first. I'm still first!

ARNALL (*To* MOLLY)　Bitch. Bitch. You bitch!

STEPHEN (*To* ARNALL)　You're second. You were nowhere.
　　You were nowhere.

FLEMING　What happened?

ARNALL　He hit me.

FLEMING　Yeah. I saw him hit you. What happened?
　　　　(*In the meantime* DOLAN *and* MOLLY *are dancing on
　　　　the floor, stage right of the line.* DOLAN *sings. Note
　　　　that after each "dance,"* MOLLY *calmly returns and
　　　　brushes her hair*)

31

DOLAN (*Sings*)
>I want a girl just like the girl
>Who married dear old dad.
>>(*He sings and then repeats the song, slowly at first, and then in an ever-increasing pace until a conclusion. Over his song, the dialogue continues, after everyone in line does a "take"*)

FLEMING   This is terrible. I forgot to move up.

STEPHEN   You didn't move up. You didn't move in. Fleming, you disappoint me. I'm tired and I'm going to sleep. I have a letter to read.
>(*He lays down on the floor and begins to read*)

FLEMING (*To* ARNALL)   You just let your old lady do that? I mean, does she do it all the time?

ARNALL   All the time. All the time.

FLEMING   That's terrible. That's a terrible thing. You must get embarrassed.

ARNALL   It doesn't hurt any more. Not after all these years.

FLEMING   Why don't you throw her out?

ARNALL   Why? She's predictable.

FLEMING   Predictable?

ARNALL   Consistent. I never have any surprises with Molly. She's pure. All bad.

FLEMING   That's good?

ARNALL Surprises hurt. You should know that. Look how hurt you were when you didn't move up. Or "move in." You were surprised and hurt, right?

FLEMING That's bad.
(MOLLY *and* DOLAN *finish as* DOLAN *screams*)

DOLAN Dad! Dad! Dad!

ARNALL Right. My philosophy is quite simple. Never ever leave yourself open for surprise, and you'll never be surprised. Surprise brings pain, pain is bad. No surprise, no pain. No pain, no bad. No bad, all good. (*Proudly*) I've got it made. They're finished now. Want to take a whack at it?

FLEMING What?

ARNALL Go on. Go ahead. Have a bash. Have a go at it. It'll do you good. Go on. I don't mind.

FLEMING You sure?

ARNALL Positive.

FLEMING Do you mind if Dolan holds my place in line?

ARNALL Of course not.

FLEMING Hey, Dolan.

DOLAN What?

FLEMING Hold my place in line, will you? I'd like to have a go at it.

33

DOLAN Have a what?

FLEMING Have a bash. That's what her old man calls it. Hey, Dolan. Hold my place will you?

DOLAN (*Crawls wearily to* FLEMING's *place and falls there*) Go get it.
> (FLEMING *stares at* DOLAN, MOLLY, ARNALL *and the lot again. He grabs* MOLLY *and drags her upstage slightly, then jumps on top of her. He sings his song and they dance*)

FLEMING
> Take me out to the ball game,
> Take me out to the park,
> Buy me some peanuts and Crackerjacks,
> I don't care if I never get back,
> For it's . . .
>> (*As he continues his song, the dialogue does not stop*)

DOLAN I like the way you think, Arnold.

ARNALL You mean my little philosophy?

DOLAN Yeah. I guess you could call it that. Your little philosophy. I like the way you think, Arnold.

ARNALL Ar*nall*. (*Spells it*) A-R-N-A-L-L. My mother wanted to call me Arthur. My father liked Nathan. Thought it was strong. My grandmother liked Lloyd, after Harold Lloyd. So they took the A-R from Arthur, the N-A from Nathan, the L-L from Lloyd, and called me Arnall. What do you want?

34

DOLAN I overheard your little philosophy and I want to tell you how touched I was. I have a little philosophy myself. I call it the Under*dog* Philosophy.

ARNALL Under*dog?*
(DOLAN *takes* ARNALL *by the arm, circles him around and quietly walks into* second *place*)

DOLAN Underdog. You notice that I'm second in line, right?

ARNALL Right.
(DOLAN *has now come full circle around and holds* second!)

DOLAN You notice that I was second to make it with your wife—second in this line to make it—right?

ARNALL Right.

DOLAN There you are.

ARNALL I don't get it.

DOLAN Haven't you ever heard of Arnold Palmer? He's the world's richest golfer. He always looks like he's going to lose. All the time. Then he quietly ends up first. All the time. But everybody always looks at him and remembers that he always almost loses. They forget that he almost never loses. So they root for him. He's the underdog. But he's the world's richest golfer.

ARNALL I still don't get it.

DOLAN Everybody wants to be first, right?

ARNALL   Right.
          (DOLAN *has succeeded by walking confused* ARNALL
          into third)

DOLAN   Okay. Now you can be obvious about it. Just jump
right in like the kid and yell and brag about being first.
Or about deserving to be first. Or you can stand back a
little. Maybe in second place—for a while. When nobody's looking, you kind of sneak into first place. But first
you have to build up everybody's confidence that you're
really one hell of a nice guy. You smile a lot. Say nice
things all the time, like, "Great night for a line, huh?" or,
"Terrific wife you got there, Arnall, kid." And then, when
everybody likes you, you sneak up. Quick. Into first
place.

ARNALL   Why do you call that *underdog?*

DOLAN   The easiest way to kick a dog in the balls is to be
underneath him. Let him walk on top of you for a while,
take a good aim, and . . . (*Yells*) WAM!

ARNALL   I get it.
          (STEPHEN *looks up sharply as* DOLAN *yells*)

STEPHEN   What's that noise?

DOLAN   Love.

ARNALL   They're in love.

STEPHEN (*Stares out at* MOLLY)   He's in love with *her?*

DOLAN   Her. His terrific wife.

36

ARNALL   Don't argue. I can't stand the noise. I've got a headache.

STEPHEN   There's a beer in Fleming's sack. He won't miss it. Get the beer.

DOLAN (*Finds it*)   There are a hundred beers in Fleming's sack. How long do you figure he figured to be here?

STEPHEN   Don't count. Pass the beer.

DOLAN (*Passing them out*)   A hundred beers. Maybe a hundred and fifty. That's a hell of a lot.

ARNALL   That is a lot.

STEPHEN (*Drinking*)   A toast. A toast to the God of Non-pasteurization!

ARNALL (*Drinks*)   Nonpasteurization?

DOLAN   A pork chop in every can. Jesus Christ.

STEPHEN   What's the matter?

DOLAN   Fleming's got a hundred and fifty pork chops in here.

ARNALL   My philosophy is quite simple. Never ever leave yourself open for surprise and you'll never be surprised. Surprise brings pain. Pain is bad. No surprise, no pain. No pain, no bad. No bad, all good. (*Proudly*) I've got it made. (*He begins to cry*) I've got it made. I've got it made.

37

DOLAN Take it easy, pal. Have a drink. Go on. You've got a terrific wife.

ARNALL Don't touch me. Leave me be.

STEPHEN (*Fiercely*) Leave him be. Go on, Dolan. Let go of him. It isn't fair, Dolan. It just isn't fair. Leave him be.
   (STEPHEN *holds his letter. He's been weeping*)

DOLAN (*Shocked by* STEPHEN's *anger*) Okay, okay, kid. (*To* ARNALL) Take it easy, pal. It's a great night for a line. Easy does it.

ARNALL I can't understand it, not at all. My philosophy is so simple. So simple. I've got it made. Why am I so damned miserable?
   (FLEMING's *song cuts through now*)

FLEMING (*Singing*)
   Take me out to the ball game,
   Take me out to the park,
   Buy me some peanuts and Crackerjacks.
   I don't care if I never get back.
   For it's root, root, root for the hometeam.
   If they don't win it's a shame.
   For it's one, two, three and you're out
   At the old ball game . . .
      (*He repeats and his song fades under the dialogue again*)

ARNALL (*Steps forward, as in a dream*) At first it was all a terrible surprise. I worked all the time. I was away all the time. I knew she had friends, but I thought they were just friends. I didn't know that they were . . . that they were . . .

38

That they were what?

ARNALL (*Back to* DOLAN) That they were screwing her, for Christ's sake!

DOLAN Oh, that. What did you think they were doing?

ARNALL It was all a terrible surprise. That's why I developed my philosophy. I have a real philosophy, for Christ's sake. A real philosophy. I'm supposed to be gleeful. All the time.

DOLAN (*Checking* FLEMING) They'll be done soon. Great night for a line. Terrific wife you've got there, Arnall, kid.

ARNALL Christ, I can't stand it! I just can't stand it.
(ARNALL *pulls* FLEMING *off of* MOLLY *and jumps on her himself.* FLEMING *is, as always, stunned*)

FLEMING Hey, I didn't finish. I didn't finish. (*To* DOLAN) I didn't finish. I didn't finish!

DOLAN Hop in Line. You can be up third.

FLEMING But I didn't finish! Didn't you see?

DOLAN See? Of course I saw. You were doing it with that guy's old lady. Right in front of his eyes, you jerk. Of course I saw.

FLEMING *You* did it in front of his eyes.

DOLAN Jesus, don't remind me.

FLEMING I didn't finish. For Christ's sake, I'm hornier than ever.

39

STEPHEN   What took you so long?

FLEMING   Shut up, kid. Shut up before I finish with *you*.

ARNALL   Molly. It's me. Arnall. Your husband.

MOLLY (*Shocked*)   Arnall? What the hell are you doing?

ARNALL   I'm doing it. With you. My wife. A surprise, Molly! A surprise!

MOLLY   You've lost your place in line. You stepped out of line!

ARNALL   I couldn't stand it. Watching all those others doing it with you. It drove me crazy. It made me want you, Molly. I really want you.

MOLLY   Oh, Arnall. You're such a bore.

ARNALL   Please, Molly. Please.

MOLLY   Well, you're doing it, aren't you?

ARNALL   I am. Oh. I am. Oh, I like it, Molly. I like it.

MOLLY   Hurry up, Arnall. Hurry up.

ARNALL   Shall I sing?

MOLLY   Just hurry up, Arnall. Just hurry up.

ARNALL (*Singing*)
    Happy birthday to you,
    Happy birthday to you,
    Happy birthday, dear Molly,

Happy birth~~d~~ you.
    (*He repeats the song under dialogue*)

DOLAN   Now that's the way it should be. A man and his
wife. That's a beautiful thing. Great night, huh?
    (STEPHEN, *helping* ARNALL *and* MOLLY *gain speed,
sings his wallet*)

STEPHEN   Sak's card and a Hertz card and an Avis card and
a UN-*ih*-Card Card and a Diners Club and a Chemical
New York.

DOLAN   That's a beautiful sight, isn't it?

FLEMING   It's terrible. *Terrible.* I never finished,

DOLAN   Just wait, Fleming. Let the husband finish first.
That's decent enough. Then you can finish. You can start
from scratch.

MOLLY   Hurry up, Arnall.

FLEMING   Yeah, Arnall. Hurry up.
    (ARNALL's *erection and song begin to "die" offstage*)

STEPHEN (*Sings*)   That one's dead. That one's dead. That
one's dead. That one's dead.

DOLAN   Sing a happy song, kid. For Christ's sake. That part
of your wallet depresses the hell out of me.

STEPHEN (*He sings again*)   Henry Brown, insurance man.
Harry Schwartz the tailor. Alvin Krantz, delivery service.
My Uncle Max, the sailor.
    (MOLLY *and* ARNALL *bunnyhop on to stage with
gusto*)

41

DOLAN   That's nice. That's got a beat.

STEPHEN (*Continuing to sing with the same gusto*)   Franklin National Savings Bank, Papert, Koenig and Lois. (*Stops. Speaks*) He's ready! He's ready!

ARNALL (*Screams*)   Surprise, Molly! Surprise!

DOLAN   That's a beautiful thing.
(*Almost weeping.* ARNALL *collapses in* MOLLY's *arms. She calmly takes a cigarette from his pocket and smokes*)

FLEMING   Can I go now?

DOLAN   Give it another minute, Fleming. Have a beer. It's such a great night for a line. What a wife he's got!

FLEMING   Jesus. That's my beer you're drinking.
(*He sees the beer and potato chips*)

DOLAN   Drink. Don't worry.

FLEMING   My Real Draft Piels. And my Lay's.

DOLAN   You've got enough beer for everyone. What's your problem?

FLEMING   You could have asked permission, that's all. Give us a beer.

DOLAN   One for me, one for you.

STEPHEN   I'm ready for another beer. Can I have a beer?

FLEMING   Give me a piece of gum and I'll give you a beer.

42

STEPHEN   Fair enough.
      (*He hands him half a stick of chewing gum.* FLEM-
      ING *hands over a beer*)

DOLAN   Cigarette?
      (*He offers them around to all*)

ARNALL   Were you surprised, Molly?

MOLLY   Let me go, Arnall.

FLEMING   No. Not yet. Not yet. I never finished.
      (*He shoves* ARNALL *off of* MOLLY *and falls on top*)

MOLLY   Hey.

FLEMING   I never finished.

MOLLY   Take the gum out of your mouth.

FLEMING   Oh.
      (*They dance off stage*)

ARNALL   What place am I in?

DOLAN   Third.

STEPHEN   Last.

ARNALL   I'd rather be third.

STEPHEN   You're in last place.

DOLAN   Shut up, kid. Don't listen to the kid. You're third.
   Two from the front. You did very well. I watched you all
   the way.

43

ARNALL   It's been a long time. I've got to practice up a little, maybe. A little practice and I'd be better.

DOLAN   You did good.

ARNALL   I'll practice up some.

FLEMING (*Sings*)
  Take me out to the ball game,
  Take me out to the park, . . .

ARNALL   Oh, God! Him again.

DOLAN   Don't watch. Have a beer. You'll cool down. You'll feel better. Terrific wife, great night.

ARNALL   My legs are all rubbery and my stomach's sick and my head aches.

DOLAN   Lay down.

ARNALL (*Drops like a rock*)   Ohhh. I'm sick.

DOLAN   Just lay still. You'll feel okay in a minute.

FLEMING (*Continues his song at a more rapid speed*)
  Buy me some peanuts and Crackerjacks,
  I don't care if I never get back . . .

DOLAN   You feeling any better now?

ARNALL (*Screams*)   I want it again.

DOLAN   You what?

ARNALL   I want it again. Molly's mine. I want it again. I liked it.

DOLAN   You'll get sick again, pal. You know it makes you sick.

ARNALL   I like it. I like it.

DOLAN   Fleming. . (*No answer*) Fleming! (*No answer*) Fleming.
> (DOLAN *reaches over with his foot and kicks* FLEMING *a hard one in the behind.* FLEMING *jumps up*)

FLEMING   What's the matter?

DOLAN   Her old man wants it again.

FLEMING   He had it already.

DOLAN   He wants it again.

STEPHEN   He wants it again.

FLEMING   I heard Dolan.

DOLAN   He wants it again.

ARNALL   I want it again.

FLEMING (*To* MOLLY)   Your old man wants it again.

MOLLY   I want the boy.

DOLAN   But your old man wants it.

MOLLY   I want the boy.

DOLAN   She wants you.

STEPHEN I heard her.

MOLLY I want you, boy.

STEPHEN I heard you.

ARNALL She likes them young.

FLEMING What about me?

DOLAN You had two chances.

FLEMING I didn't finish.

DOLAN You had two chances.

FLEMING I was almost finished. Some bastard kicked me.

DOLAN Two chances. I only had one. The kid only had one.

FLEMING The kid took two.

DOLAN Two on one chance. *He's a kid.*

ARNALL She likes the young ones. She always likes the young ones.

MOLLY Come here, boy.

STEPHEN (*Pretends to be engrossed in his wallet*) American Express. Chemical New York. Unicard. This one's dead. This one's dead. This one's dead. My library card!
(DOLAN *pushes* STEPHEN *violently at* MOLLY. STEPHEN *falls upon her.* DOLAN *jumps up into first position.* FLEMING *jumps over* ARNALL)

46

DOLAN I'm first! I'm first.

STEPHEN You made me lose my place.

MOLLY You have such a wonderful bone structure.

ARNALL She always always likes them young.

STEPHEN (*Sings, with a shrug*)
Should he, for instance, wish to go dancing,
He'll face the music, I'll lead the band, yes,
I'll lead the band.
And then I'll take my cue, without ado,
And slyly, very, very, very, very, very slyly,
Using discretion, I shall uncover his secret plan.
Subtly outwitting, innocent seeming,
Cleverly hitting, planning and scheming,
I'll get the best of the hypocrite yet,
I'll get him yet!

ARNALL I'm last, last, last. *Last damnit!*

DOLAN Tell him he's third. (*To* FLEMING) Tell him he's third.

FLEMING You're third.

ARNALL I'm last. There are only three of us. One, two, three. Three is me. I'm last.

DOLAN Two on the street. Those two. The kid and your terrific wife.

FLEMING That makes five.

DOLAN   You're two from the front and two from the back. Two from first and two from last. You're the average.
(STEPHEN *sings and he and* MOLLY *dance.* ARNALL *tells his story to the world*)

ARNALL   I would like to tell the story of my marriage. I worked hard every night. I knew she had friends, but I never knew they were doing it. (*Pauses*) That's the story of my marriage.

DOLAN   As first man, I say that Arnall gets a chance to do it again as soon as the kid is finished. (STEPHEN *screams the ending to his song*) The kid is finished.

FLEMING   Have a bash, Arnall.

ARNALL   I'll lose my place in Line. Never mind.

DOLAN   Stay put, then. Fleming? You want a third, uh, try?

FLEMING   I'm second. It ain't worth it now. You want another one, Dolan? Huh? Why don't you have a go at it?

DOLAN   You're pretty obvious, Fleming. Pretty obvious.

STEPHEN   (*Screams and jumps into the air*) The line's facing the wrong way. The line's facing the wrong way.
(*They all turn around to see where he's looking.* STEPHEN *grabs* MOLLY, *using her as a ram, jams her into second position and recaptures first for himself. He and* MOLLY *kiss a fantastic kiss*)

DOLAN   I'm third.

FLEMING   I'm fourth.

ARNALL   I'm last. I'm really last now.

DOLAN   That was filthy rotten, kid.

FLEMING   That kid is no good. I told you that that kid was no good.

DOLAN   Jesus. Jesus Christ. I'm going to get you, kid. I'm going to get you.

STEPHEN   Don't hurt the lady. Watch where you push. (*Pushes* MOLLY *violently into* DOLAN. *Sings to* DOLAN)
   La capriolo le insegnero! . . .
   (DOLAN *backs down, meekly*) That's my victory song my mother taught me.

MOLLY   I hate your mother.

STEPHEN   You don't know her.

MOLLY   I'm jealous of her. You love her, so I hate her.

STEPHEN   Don't hate my mother. She couldn't help herself. None of them can. I wrote to her once. Not just to her. That's not my problem. To both of them. To all of them. "Dear folks," I wrote. "I'm sorry I'm such a bastard for not writing before tonight—and I'll never know really why I chose tonight to write, really write, after all this time has passed—but I must ask you if the trees are still so tall the tops go out of sight? When I hold a cookie behind my back and a speck of it in my right hand in front of me for the dog—whose dog was that?—does the dog still creep around behind me and eat the big piece? Does a football still hurt with its weight and size so enormous, one wonders what the sport of it is anyway? Do I still beat up Bobby all the time because he's the only one on earth I can really beat up? Is "The Secret Garden" still on downtown on Fridays at the Community House? If it is, let's all go next Friday. Afterwards we'll get sick on hot-fudge sundaes and we'll all call Bobby and give him some of our fudge and all say we're sorry and give that dog the whole cookie this time and just keep a speck for ourselves. I love you. Your son, Stephen." I got a letter back saying, "Stephen, have you gone crazy? Come home right away."

(STEPHEN *is almost weeping now*)

FLEMING   You should have listened. They were right. You are crazy.

STEPHEN   Of course they were right. Of course I'm crazy.

MOLLY   No you're not. Stop it, Fleming.

STEPHEN   It's a game you can't win. Victory comes when they take off their clothes and come running at you screaming WE LOVE YOU! WE LOVE YOU! And you jump out the window in terror. (*Laughs*) Don't hate her. The letter came this morning. This morning. "Are you crazy?" Yes! I'm crazy! Crazy enough to get into one last line. To start one last line. And watch the fools line up. Thinking that they're feeling something. Seeing something. (*Pauses*) You're just distractions. Distractions. (*Pauses*) You see nothing. You can't see a thing.

MOLLY   I see you. I felt you.

STEPHEN   What do you see?

MOLLY   You have beautiful bones.

STEPHEN   My bones? Bones? That's all you saw?

MOLLY   I know what I see.

STEPHEN   What you see! What you see! You haven't seen anything. You haven't seen what's happening . . . what's happening. The Feast of Stephen . . . that's what's happening. And you haven't seen a speck of it. You're too God damned interested in your bones and your movie stars. (*To the world*) Are the stars still mine? Does the sun still follow me wherever I go? Can I grab quickly in the pond where a bullfrog was, and still find that bullfrog squirming and frightened . . . in my hand? Squirming and frightened until I realize that he's so much smaller than Bobby even, it's no fair at all, so I throw him back in the water and he swims away with the sun on him, for a second, and then deep below, where there are only dead kids who fell through in the winter and vines that pull you down and hold you? Oh, my God! Is any of it there at all? Has anything stayed pretty and gentle and easy and simple and soft and warm? (*Screams, almost crying*) Answer me! Is there anything that might love me a little? (*Changes his posture to false bravado*) "Dear Stephen. Have you gone crazy? Come home right away!" Home? Home? Where the hell is home? (*Back to* MOLLY) Oh, sure. You see. You feel. You hear. Well, hear this. One hour ago I was playing a little game I always lose. "Be First." This is turning out to be the great victory, Molly. The first victory for me. The first and the last. I'm going to win tonight and you're going to help me. You and all your friends.

ARNALL   You're really an evil person.

DOLAN   Shhhh. He's going batty.

51

STEPHEN Right, Arnall. For all the wrong reasons. I played badguy tonight. That's fun too. And I found out maybe that's how you win. Maybe you just go on playing badguy all the time. Until it's a real part of you. (*To* DOLAN) Did you say "batty," Dolan? There's a word. Batty. Right again. For all the wrong reasons. Batty's something to play, right along with badguy. But maybe if you play them simultaneously, you never lose. Never ever lose. All the batty, badguys win. That's kind of sensible, Dolan. Very sensible. (*To* MOLLY, *finally*) See, Molly? You see nothing.

MOLLY You have beautiful bones. Listen to me. Not everybody has beautiful bones. You do. You really do.

STEPHEN You can't see my bones. Only the shape of my bones.

MOLLY I can tell. I can tell. I love you, anyway!
    (*They all babble at once*)

ARNALL Always the young ones. I'm sick of it. Sick of it. Sick of the young ones getting to be first.

DOLAN Easy, Arnall. We'll get him.

FLEMING Not finished. Not first. We'll get him.

ARNALL Cuckolded. Cuckolded. I'm a buffoon . . . a buffoon.

STEPHEN You're all buffoons. Not just you, Arnall. All of you, fools!

MOLLY You have the face of a president. Or a senator. A Kennedy's face. A beautiful face.

(*They babble together again until* STEPHEN *cuts them off*)

FLEMING   Breathe the air now, kid. Breathe it deep. We're going to get you.

DOLAN   Third. First to third.

ARNALL   Last, really last. This time there's no question about it.

STEPHEN   Shut up, idiots. We're talking about my bones.

FLEMING   Idiots! Who are you calling "idiot"?

STEPHEN   All of you. It's simple. I'm first and anyone who isn't first is an idiot. We've got nothing in common, so why talk about it?

DOLAN   We've all got something in common, kid. And don't you forget it.

STEPHEN   What's that, Dolan?

DOLAN   We've all been at his terrific wife. Whatever she's got, we've got.

FLEMING   That's true. We're like a club. Whatever she's got, we've got. (*Does a huge "take" to* ARNALL) What's she got?

ARNALL   (*Simply*)   Molly? Nothing. She's ugly. But she's clean.

STEPHEN   They're right, damn you. You let them all have you. Even your husband.

ARNALL (*Hopefully*) Molly?

MOLLY Nobody had me.

FLEMING Nobody but all of us!

DOLAN You never finished.

FLEMING I had her all the same. Penetration is all that counts, ain't it? I penetrated.

MOLLY Nobody had me.

STEPHEN (*Turns sharply about, back to* MOLLY, *screams and weeps*) Everybody had you . . . everybody.

MOLLY Nobody had me.

DOLAN She's crazy, too. (*To* ARNALL) You've got a crazy wife, Mister.

MOLLY Nobody had me, get it? Nobody. *I* had all of you. *I* did the doing. Not you. *I* made the choices. You all wanted to be first, what kept you from it, huh? What kept you? (*Pushes* STEPHEN *over the line, out of first place, viciously. He falls to one side. Shocked*) I'm first now. *Me!*

STEPHEN (*wandering, confused*) You pushed me. She pushed me.

DOLAN She's crazy. You've got a crazy wife, Mister. This is a terrible night.

ARNALL She's *always* first. She's *always* first. The shirts.

54

The young kid. You two. Now this. She's always doing things like killing my philosophies, then ending up first.

FLEMING   You never had me, lady. I had you.

MOLLY   Did you now?

FLEMING   You bet I did. And they all saw me, too.

MOLLY   Any one of you want to punch me or kick me or throw me down on the street so you can be first? Come on. Let's see how you beat a woman.

FLEMING   Nobody's going to hit a woman. Not while I'm here.

STEPHEN   Fleming, you're pure. I couldn't have made a better last line.

MOLLY (*To* STEPHEN)   You've talked enough. Your words are nonsense. You try to confuse everybody, but not me. Not me. I can take just so much of it, Stevie. You're just a baby, crying for mommy and daddy. Just like all of them. I know what I've got. I know what my flesh means. I never had anybody when I was skinny. You know why? They're all just like you! When it comes right down to a good roll in the hay, they want to roll with mommy. And rolling in a line is all the better, 'cause daddy's watching. Daddy's going crazy with failure.

DOLAN   What kind of talk is that? You've got a crazy wife, Arnall. She's a real bitch, all right.

ARNALL   I told you so. I told you so. Surprises. I never know what she's saying. What she's going to do next.

55

STEPHEN   Don't flatter yourself, Molly. Not for a second. You've screwed your way to first and you'll be screwed right out of first. That's the way it's always been and that's the way it's always going to be. This line's my last, Molly. You really think I'm going to let you come in first?

MOLLY   I am first. I am first. And I'm not moving. I screwed my way to first and now I'm resting. Maybe this is my last line too. I know about distractions or whatever the hell you call it! Look who's first. Just look who's first. Me. Molly. Just where I knew I'd be from the moment I saw this line.

FLEMING   You got yourself a real bitch for a wife there, Arnall. A real bitch.

ARNALL   I know. I know.

MOLLY   I know what you've been thinking all night. Here we are, four big shots. One woman in line. Might as well roll her over, just to kill time. That's what you're always thinking. That's what every line's about, right? And you think in any other place you'd never give me a look . . . but . . . as long as we're all killing time together . . . why not? 'Course, under *normal* conditions, she'd never be good enough for me. Well, I've got a piece of news for you all: under any conditions, none of you is good enough for me. Not a one of you!

STEPHEN   Molly. You're good enough for me.

MOLLY   Go to the back of the line, boy. You didn't satisfy me.

STEPHEN   What are you talking about?

MOLLY Go to the back of the line. You didn't make it. You didn't thrill me. You need experience. You make love like a child.

STEPHEN What about my beautiful bones?

MOLLY Go to the back of the line.

DOLAN That's telling the wise-ass kid. Go to the back of the line, kid. You heard the lady.

MOLLY Don't gloat. Don't lick your lips like that. I could have done better with an ape than with you.

FLEMING Terrific, Molly. An ape, Dolan. An ape.

MOLLY Are you the one with the beer and the gum who's too old and tired to finish?

FLEMING What's that supposed to mean?

ARNALL Molly? Molly? Is it me?

MOLLY Don't be a bore, Arnall. You couldn't satisfy a canary.

DOLAN You've run out. If none of us satisfied you, who did?

MOLLY None of you. Simple as that. I am an unsatisfied woman still looking for a man. You all failed.

DOLAN I've had better than you, tubby, and I mean some real beauties. And they've screamed for more. Screamed for more!

MOLLY   More money? Okay. Sure. I can understand that.

FLEMING   I've had models.

DOLAN   Screw your models. I had one in a car once.

FLEMING   Yeah. You told me.

MOLLY   I'm first. I'm unsatisfied. I've had four men. One three times. One unfinished. And I'm unsatisfied.

ARNALL   Don't let her get to you. Don't let her get you going. She'll drive you all crazy. Make surprises. Ruin all your philosophies. She'll hide your shirts.

MOLLY   Arnall, you're such a bore.

STEPHEN   (*Whispers to her*)   I've got something to tell you.

MOLLY   To the back of the line, sonny. You lost. You're last . . . move.

DOLAN   You're out of line completely, kid. She's right. When the crowds come, you'll be left out all together. (STEPHEN *wanders to the back position in the line but now he's smiling*)

MOLLY   I hope there's a man in the *crowd*. One man.

ARNALL   You see what I mean? She won't let up now. Now that she's first, she'll just keep pouring it on.

DOLAN   She's worse than *my* old lady. Much worse. My old lady's a dog, but nothing like yours. Yours is the biggest dog of all. Queen dog. Yeah. She's the biggest dog of all. How'd you get stuck with her, anyway?

ARNALL   She picked me up at a party.

FLEMING   I penetrated!

MOLLY   Penetration doesn't count. Not for you. Just for me. *I* had *you*. And you were heavy.
(STEPHEN *hums "The Magic Flute"*)

ARNALL   I was at a party. The lights were dim. I felt a hand sneak between my legs. I was only fifteen. It was Molly. She taught me everything I know. I don't know anything either.

MOLLY   Arnall. Stop whining.

DOLAN   She didn't teach you much, did she?

ARNALL   She taught me how to be small. How to whine.

MOLLY   Arnall, stop whining.

STEPHEN   (*Stops humming to proclaim*)   When I make love to a woman, I never shut my eyes. Never. I watch. I watch and I listen to every movement she makes.

FLEMING   (*Embarrassed*)   Shut up.

DOLAN   (*Wants to hear* STEPHEN's *"secret"*)   You shut up, Fleming.

STEPHEN   I listen to every movement she makes. So that every time I move, I understand her response. One little wiggle to the left, one little wiggle to the right and I get a response I remember. I make notes. I have a whole loose-leaf binder filled with notes and half another filled as well. All kinds of notes. How to wiggle front and

59

back. How short women respond. How tall women respond. How certain ethnic groups respond.

MOLLY   What did you learn from me, little boy?

STEPHEN   (*His guise has worked. He knows it. He sets up his next line carefully, ready to strike. He moves into position close to* MOLLY)   Never screw an ugly, greedy, slob like you. Always to follow my natural desire. Only screw who I want, when I want. If I had followed my natural desire, I never would have screwed you. Not once. Not twice. Not three times. It was all a waste of my incredibly valuable time. That's what I wanted to tell you.

MOLLY   (*Explodes*)   You little squirt. You little jerk. (*She charges at him in a rage. He knocks her aside and regains first position.* MOLLY *is out of line*)

STEPHEN   (*With a flourish*)   Gentlemen, I am first again. (*He takes the portable tape recorder and shows it*)

FLEMING   You've really got to hand it to that kid. Go on, Dolan. Hand it to the kid.

DOLAN   (*Ruefully*)   Nice work, kid.

ARNALL   I'm not last. You're last, Molly. I'm ahead of you. You're last.
        (STEPHEN *pushes the button on his tape recorder. Mozart's "Eine Kleine Nachtmusik" begins to play softly*)

DOLAN   What the hell is that?

STEPHEN   Mozart! Mozart!

60

FLEMING   Who's Mozart?

STEPHEN   Shut up. Listen. (*The music plays on. They all listen, all confused with the exception of* STEPHEN *who comes to life: he glows and giggles*) Mozart. "*Eine Kleine Nachtmusik.*" The Allegro. He was younger than me when he wrote this. A baby.

MOLLY   I'm last.

ARNALL   I'm ahead of you.

STEPHEN   The Allegro. Then Andante. The Menuett. Then Rondo.

FLEMING   Turn off the record!

MOLLY   Turn it off!
       (*They all, except* STEPHEN, *turn and face the rear and scream*)

ALL   Turn it off . . . turn it off . . . turn it off . . . turn it off . . . turn it off . . . turn it off . . .
       (*While they scream,* STEPHEN *jumps in and out of line, weaving among them all*)

STEPHEN (*As he dances*)   I'm first. Now I'm third. Now I'm fourth. Now I'm last. First again. Anywhere I want to be. Distractions. Distraction. Now I'm first again. Second. Third. Fourth. First. (*To the machine*) Shut up.
       (*He pushes the "off" button. The music switches off*)

DOLAN   Thank God.

MOLLY   That was awful.

61

ARNALL   Awful. Just awful.

STEPHEN   Idiots! You could have been first. I stepped out. You know that? You were distracted. Totally distracted.

FLEMING   Hey! He was dancing around. First place was open all that time.

ARNALL   He was last for a moment. I remember.

MOLLY (*Softly*)   Play it again!

STEPHEN   No. I only do my tricks once.

DOLAN   Play anything. Go on, kid. Play anything.

STEPHEN   I'll play nothing. I'm all through playing. The game is over. Let's get down to the nitty-gritties. You want to be first, right?

DOLAN   You know that.

STEPHEN   But you all can't be first, can you? In fact, none of you can be first. You know why? Because *I'm* first. Just me. I'm a genius and you're all idiots. I'm a genius!

DOLAN   You were lucky.

MOLLY (*Walks to* STEPHEN *and whispers seductively*)   I take back what I said, Stephen. Do you forgive me?

STEPHEN   Forgive *you?* What's to forgive with an idiot like you? (*Archly*) Back in line with the idiots.

DOLAN   Don't push your luck, kid.

STEPHEN You're dumb, Dolan. You're all dumb. You've always been dumber and you're getting dumber.

FLEMING I've waited a long time to be first, kid. Don't push your luck.

STEPHEN Idiots! You could all wait until the moon went away. Until the moon and the sun and all the stars disappeared . . . and little mice in green sneakers ran around the sky instead . . . and you know what? You'd never be first. Not any of you. You've never been first, have you? You're never going to be, either. You know that, don't you?

ARNALL We're much older than you are, son. You could show some respect.

STEPHEN Maybe I hate you most, Arnall. Just maybe. 'Cause just maybe in some berserk way, you're the one who really wrote that letter I got today. (*Like a bullet*) You're a fairy, Arnall!

ARNALL Don't push your luck, kid!

STEPHEN Push my luck! Luck? This isn't luck, it's genius. Genius! I've played this game five hundred times before, but tonight is mine. (*Sits and eats potato chips. Very flip*) I beat all of you, not with luck, but with genius. And now I'll beat Mozart, too. You know what that means? First. First for the first time. I'll die younger. The youngest. The best. First!

ARNALL He's crazy!
(STEPHEN *switches the music on and then throws the recorder on the ground. They fumble, distracted*)

STEPHEN   And after I win, you'll find out you can take it with you. *I* can take it with *me!* You'll see!
(STEPHEN *picks up the line and "eats" it*)

ARNALL (*After he steps on the tape recorder, "killing" it as though he were stepping on an insect*)   You *are* crazy!!! You are an evil, evil person.

STEPHEN   How dare you, you cuckolded little nothing! You let your wife—your fat horrible nothing wife— screw on the street while you do nothing more than watch. She screws and you watch. And tomorrow you'll crawl in bed beside her with your sweaty little body begging for a whore's kisses!

MOLLY   You animal! You animal! Arnall. Hit him!

ARNALL   Me?

DOLAN   Hit him, Fleming.

STEPHEN (*He laughs maniacally*)   I can take it with me.

ARNALL   You son of a bitch. You son of a bitch!

FLEMING   Hit him. Somebody hit him.
(STEPHEN *reveals that the line is gone. They all stop and jump back one step*)

STEPHEN   What's wrong? Why are you stopping? Hit me. Kick me. Come on. Somebody's got to kill me. What's wrong?
(DOLAN *has noticed that they are all so undone by their confusion that they are no longer paying attention to first place. He jumps into first position, but of course the line is gone.* DOLAN *is astonished*)

DOLAN   Hey! Where's the line?

FLEMING   The line! Where is it?

ARNALL   The line!

MOLLY   Arnall! The line's gone.

ARNALL   Where'd it go?

STEPHEN (*Burps a little, smiles*)   I ate it.

FLEMING   What?

STEPHEN   I ate it.
   (*He groans*)

MOLLY   He ate it. He ate it?

FLEMING   He ate it. He ate it?

DOLAN   He ate it?

ARNALL   He *ate* it?

STEPHEN   I ate it. Now somebody's got to kill me. Come
on.

MOLLY   He wants us to kill him.

STEPHEN   Somebody's got to kill me! Come on!

MOLLY   See? I'm right. He *is* crazy. He's really crazy.

FLEMING   I told you that, lady. I told you that the second
you walked up. He's really crazy.

STEPHEN   What is this? I'm supposed to die!
(*He's stunned, as it appears that he isn't going to die after all*)

MOLLY   He wanted us to beat him so he'd die so there'd be a dead kid in first. And we were supposed to just watch.

ARNALL   How could we watch a thing like that?

FLEMING   Why not? We've been watching everything else.

MOLLY   Oh, my God! What if I'm pregnant?

ARNALL   Pregnant? Molly. A son? A son, Molly?

FLEMING   But I didn't finish!

MOLLY   He finished. The way it counts. What if I'm pregnant?

FLEMING   You see, Arnall? They never really forget the first one.

ARNALL   What?

DOLAN   Jesus! What a wife you've got there. What a rotten night! (*To* STEPHEN) Give us back the line, kid. They're going to open soon and we need a line.

MOLLY   They'll open and we won't have a line. (*Steps behind* STEPHEN) And I'm only second.

ARNALL   I'm right beside you.

FLEMING   Me too.

DOLAN   For crying out loud! We're all second!

FLEMING   This looks very phoney. Give us back our line, Steve

MOLLY   Please, Stephie. Please.

ARNALL   Give it back, Steven.

DOLAN   Cough it up, *Stephen,* Steve, Stevie. Cough it up.
        (STEPHEN *begins to gag and choke. The line begins to appear*)

FLEMING   Hey. The line.
        (STEPHEN *gags up the line in five pieces*)

DOLAN   There it is!

MOLLY   The line.

ARNALL   He *did* eat it.

DOLAN   He took it with him.
        (*They all freeze, as* STEPHEN *rises, dazzled*)

STEPHEN   I didn't take it with me. I didn't go anywhere. Damn it all. I'm not dead.
        (STEPHEN *begins to go through a series of contortions as a woman in labor. He gags up a piece of line.* DOLAN *grabs the first piece*)

DOLAN   I'm first. I had to wait for my chance, but I'm first. Had to wait. Wait. Hang back. But I'm first.

(DOLAN *rushes downstage left with his scrap of line and places it on the floor, standing behind it.* STEPHEN *gags again*)

FLEMING (*Grabs the line and stares at it as a moron might, then follows* DOLAN's *example, setting his line upstage left*) I'm first! Finally, I'm first! I should be first. I was the first one here. Fair's fair.
   (STEPHEN *retches as he stands up.* MOLLY *steps forward and kisses* STEPHEN *full on the lips. She comes away with a piece of line as her reward.* STEPHEN *is now a dispenser. He walks mechanically, emitting sounds like a berserk Coca-Cola machine*)

MOLLY He gave me first. He made me first. He gave me first place.
   (*She places her line downstage right. They all stare, dreamy-eyed with victory.* ARNALL *slaps* STEPHEN *on the back and a line falls into his hands*)

ARNALL (*After placing his line upstage right*) Molly. Darling. I'm first. I didn't want to be first. I never wanted first. But I'm first. And I like it, Molly. First is good.
   (STEPHEN *still walks as a machine, puking up a final scrap of line. He grabs it and just as he places it on the floor downstage center, he sees the others in their blissful stance of victory. He understands at once, laughs ironically. As he starts to run into the audience in complete liberation, the lights black out. Curtain*)

it's called

the /

sugar

plum

It's Called the Sugar Plum: John Pleshette as WALLACE
ZUCKERMAN and Marsha Mason as JOANNA DIBBLE.

IT'S CALLED THE SUGAR PLUM *was first presented as a staged reading at the Eugene O'Neill Memorial Theatre Foundation, Waterford, Connecticut, on July 18, 1967, with the following cast:*

(*In order of appearance*)

WALLACE ZUCKERMAN   Danny Goldman
JOANNA DIBBLE   Linda Segal

Staged by   Melvin Bernhardt

Subsequently, IT'S CALLED THE SUGAR PLUM *was presented by Ruth Newton Productions on January 17, 1968, at the Astor Place Theatre, New York City, on a double bill with* The Indian Wants the Bronx, *with the following cast:*

(*In order of appearance*)

WALLACE ZUCKERMAN   John Pleshette
JOANNA DIBBLE   Marsha Mason

Directed by   James Hammerstein

Setting: A cramped, one-room flat in Cambridge, Massachusetts.

Time: Late afternoon, the present.

The setting is a dormitory-styled one-room student's flat in Cambridge, Massachusetts.

The furnishing is scruffy, secondhand. A wooden table with three chairs is set stage left, a single bed, stage right. The walls are covered with mementos of college life: a school blanket, odd photographs, etc. A second bed is used for storage of books, etc. There are some books and magazines scattered about. A stack of newspapers is on the table.

WALLACE ZUCKERMAN *scans the newspapers. He is twenty-two years old, rather thin, dressed with a planned sloppiness. He studies the newspapers carefully, stopping to reread articles, snips them out, and pastes them into a scrapbook.*

A transistor radio is heard in the background. The curtains open in blackout . . . music, and then a commercial interrupts. The ANNOUNCER's *voice is heard faintly. The radio is covered by newspapers.*

Lights begin to fade, the action is seen as described above.

ANNOUNCER How much meat do you think you can get for $39.95? Ten pounds? Twenty pounds? Boston Freezer Plan gives you more meat than you ever believed possible! That's right, folks. For just $39.95 Boston Freezer Plan will give you more meat than your butcher. . . .

(ZUCKERMAN *finds and picks up the radio and switches stations quickly, so there is an interdispers-*

ing of the radio commercial with bits of the news broadcast and music. He checks his wrist watch. On cue there is a thunk at the door, as a newspaper is thrown against it. He carries the radio to the door, opens the door quickly, snatches the newspaper, shuts the door and locks it. As he begins to scan the front page of the newspaper, the commercial ends with)

NEW ANNOUNCER . . . dollars down, just ten extra pennies a day, Boston Freezer Plan will supply a spanking new Rhotostatic twenty-eight-cubic-foot freezer right in your kitchen or pantry.

(He switches the dial again)

ANNOUNCER There is speculation that the soil purchased last month to refertilize the Common is the very soil that's been missing.

(He switches the dial again. Music is heard)

SINGERS "Lonely streets, lonely streets, lonelier when you're all alone. Lovely when you want to be alone . . ."

(He switches the dial once more, then scans the front page again, setting the radio on the table)

NEW ANNOUNCER Don't even think once. Call your good neighbor from . . . *(a chorus sings)* "Boston Freezer . . . that's the Plan!"

(Just as ZUCKERMAN is about to turn the page, the newscaster comes back on)

ANNOUNCER Cambridge. Frank Weeks Simpson, nineteen . . . *(ZUCKERMAN throws down the newspaper and runs to the radio, kneeling, he turns up the volume)* was pronounced dead on arrival last night at Massachusetts General Hospital. He was run down and killed as he

78

slipped under the wheels of a passing automobile on Mount Auburn Street in Cambridge. The pavement was wet from last night's heavy rainfall and Simpson, riding a skateboard, slipped and fell, just as the moving car was upon him. The driver of the car was twenty-two-year-old Harvard student Wallace Zuckerman.

(*The* ANNOUNCER *pronounces Zuckerman like "sucker-man."* ZUCKERMAN *corrects the radio, pronouncing Zuckerman like "Zoo-ker-man"*)

ZUCKERMAN Zookerman.

ANNOUNCER The tragedy was witnessed by Judge Herman Lee of the Cambridge District Court. Judge Lee issued a statement at the scene of the accident that Zuckerman—

ZUCKERMAN (*Corrects the radio again*) Zookerman.

ANNOUNCER . . . was not, repeat, *not* speeding and not at fault. Judge Lee again confirmed his statement this morning and suggested the formation of an official committee banning the use of skateboards on the streets of Cambridge. A date has not as yet been set for the final hearing. Zuckerman—

ZUCKERMAN (*Correcting this time in disgust*) Zookerman!

ANNOUNCER . . . released without bail, faces a possible, but highly improbable, manslaughter charge. Worcester. A fire swept through the deserted Wearever Knitting Mills early this morning—

(ZUCKERMAN *switches dials one last time. Music again*)

79

SINGERS "Lonely streets, lonely streets, lovely when you want to be alone."

(ZUCKERMAN *switches off the radio. He walks to his scrapbook and pastes two more clippings on to one of the blank pages. Suddenly there is a knock at the door. The knock is ferocious, loud.* ZUCKERMAN *springs to his feet and looks about the room carefully. He takes two steps and then freezes in one position. The knock sounds again, even louder than before.* ZUCKERMAN *begins to talk, but his words are barely audible*)

ZUCKERMAN Who is it? (*He clears his throat, then tries again*) Who is it? (*There is silence.* ZUCKERMAN *moves to the door, quietly. He steps back, puzzled and frightened. He looks about his room once more, without moving. The knock sounds again, incredibly loud, almost as if the door might be kicked in any moment.* ZUCKERMAN *is clearly shaken. He attempts to speak again, but his voice cracks, weaker than the first time*) Can I help you? (*Clears his throat*) Can you help me? (*Silence again*) Who is it? (*There is no answer*) Who's there? (*Still no answer. He walks to the door and calls again*) Yes? (*No answer*) I hear you, who are you? Who's there? (*He cracks open the door cautiously, as* JOANNA DIBBLE *enters. She sweeps into the room, wearing black tights, black skirt, black sweater, black shoes. A fraternity pin is pinned to her sweater. She is wide-eyed, with long straight hair.* JOANNA *is* ZUCKERMAN'S *age*) Joanna Dibble, right?

JOANNA (*Enraged*) Killer! Murderer!

ZUCKERMAN Jesus, I'm sorry. It was an accident . . .

JOANNA (*Stepping in closer*) So this is what a killer looks like. Fascinating. You don't even show any signs of a tear. Killer. Murderer. Not even a tear. Killer-murderer. Not even a tear.

ZUCKERMAN I cried all night.

JOANNA You're free! It's incredible! You're free! They didn't beat you. They didn't lock you up. You're free.

ZUCKERMAN He was on a skateboard. He slipped under the car. It wasn't my fault. There was a witness. He slipped.

JOANNA Oh, my God! He slipped under the car. That sets you free. That excuses you. That lets you wander the streets tonight. And tomorrow. (*Pauses*) Tell me something, Zuckerman.

ZUCKERMAN (*Corrects her pronunciation*) Zookerman . . .

JOANNA Tell me something, killer. What sets me free? What sets me free?

ZUCKERMAN You're not arrested for anything.

JOANNA (*Her act runs out of gas*) Arrested? Of course I'm not arrested. It's not a crime to be in love. It's not a crime to give yourself totally to another. It's not even a crime, it seems, to drive your car over a man's body. Oh, God. What sets me free?

ZUCKERMAN Here. Sit down.
    (*He offers the chair*)

81

JOANNA (*Not noticing*) The plans. The dreams. The *commitment!* (*As if a revelation*) How about the commitment. It was total. Total. Did you know that we were getting married in May, right after graduation?

ZUCKERMAN No.

JOANNA Well, now you know. Now you know. And you can stand there facing me as though I've come for tea. As though I've come to borrow a pencil. Or a cup of . . . something. Jesus, God! Are you flesh, or are you a machine? (*As the scene plays, she forces him to walk backwards as she attacks. Finally, he trips and falls to the floor*) How symbolic. How symbolic. Why don't I have my car now. I could drive over your body. I could drive right over you and squeeze the life out of you. Oh. Oh. (*She cries . . . and cries*)

ZUCKERMAN Oh, please, Joanna. Sit down. You'll feel better. I'll get you a cup of coffee. You want a cup of coffee?

JOANNA (*Whimpers*) Yes. Please. I promised I wouldn't cry. Yes.

ZUCKERMAN (*Remembering*) I don't have any coffee. You want some water? (*No response*) Peanut butter?

JOANNA (*Without looking at him*) We were getting married in May. May twentieth or so. You know that?

ZUCKERMAN Joanna, it was an accident. An accident. I wasn't speeding or anything. He fell right under my car. He slipped. He could have fallen under anybody's car. Even your car.

JOANNA (*Looks at him*) I don't have a car.

82

ZUCKERMAN   If you did, he could have. Anybody's.

JOANNA   Then why yours? Why yours?

ZUCKERMAN (*To God*)   That's what I've been asking myself all night. Why mine?

JOANNA   It means nothing, does it? An accident. Anybody's car. So you're free and I'm alone. My commitment is gone. My love is gone. My life is gone.

ZUCKERMAN   You're young, Joanna. You're young. There'll be others.

JOANNA (*Rises, in a rage*)   That's what they all say. That's what they all say. You, too? You, too? Even the one who kills? That's what you say, too?

ZUCKERMAN (*Flustered*)   I didn't mean it the way it sounded.

JOANNA   What do you mean, then? What do you mean? You think I'll love again? You think my life will continue? With what? Why? My life. My work. It's ended.

ZUCKERMAN   You work?

JOANNA   That's gone, too.

ZUCKERMAN   Where do you work?

JOANNA   My painting. My career. It's over now. There's no reason to continue.

ZUCKERMAN   I saw two of your paintings in the Common —in the Arts Festival. One was a play poster, right? Hey,

83

that's right. I saw you in a play, too. The one about the lesbian. You were terrific.

JOANNA (*Stronger than ever*)   So you know. You've seen my work. You killed *that*, too. How do you feel about the fact that you've killed *that* as well? Are you crying now? Are there tears welling up in your eyes?

ZUCKERMAN (*Long pause. He's rattled at this point and slightly annoyed*)   Just what the hell are you talking about?

JOANNA   My career, killer. You didn't just run over a *thing* last night. You didn't snuff out a candle. You killed more than one person. You killed *two*, Zuckerman. You drove your car over two lives!

ZUCKERMAN   Look, Miss Dibble, I didn't . . .

JOANNA (*Hates her name. Simply*)   Call me Joanna.

ZUCKERMAN   Look, Joanna. I didn't kill anybody. That's not what I mean. Yeah. Sure. I killed whatshisname, Simpson. And I know he was your husband. I mean he was gonna be your husband. And I'm sorry. *I Goddamned well am sorry!* But it was an accident. An accident. You think I'm just a clod without a heart.

JOANNA   Yes!

ZUCKERMAN (*Does a take and continues*)   I was the one who did it. *I'm* the one who's got to remember what the wheels sounded like. What the cops accused me of. *I'm* the one who's got to suffer for all of that. It hurts *me* too, you know.

(*And that's* ZUCKERMAN's *strength, exhausted for the moment, as* JOANNA *recoups her position for the attack*)

JOANNA   You heard the wheels. You heard the wheels. Oh, Jesus Christ. YOU heard the wheels! And you suffer. You poor suffering bastard. You *poor* suffering bastard. My heart is yours. I feel only pity. (*Pauses*) You skinny little fink. You took your Goddamned car and murdered my man . . . yes, my *man!* You think I run around falling in love every day? Frank and I had been pinned for five months. Five months. Five whole months of my life snuffed out. Five months burned away. A life is gone. A career is gone. Yes, a career! Who do you think I worked for? For myself? Hah! You've seen my painting. Was that the work of a child? Hah! That was the work of a woman. A whole woman. Not a child, but a woman in love. Love.

ZUCKERMAN   (*Fiercely—he musters all his energy*)   Shut up! That's right. Shut up and listen to me.
(*She starts for the door. He runs quickly and blocks her exit*)

JOANNA   Let me out of here, you pig. Let me out of here.

ZUCKERMAN   (*Screams*)   No. No, God damn it! Not until you've heard me! (*As she tries to push him aside, he picks up a chair and motions as though he might hit her with it. She pulls back. He slams the chair down in front of the door, sits in it himself, blocking the door*) Now shut up!

JOANNA   What are you going to do?

85

ZUCKERMAN I'm going to talk. Just for a minute. You're going to listen. Then you can go.

JOANNA Why are you doing this?

ZUCKERMAN (*Strongly, but indeed frightened*) Because you've got to listen to me. Please, Joanna. Please. I'm begging you. Please listen to me.

JOANNA What could *you* say? What do you *want*?

ZUCKERMAN Miss Dibble, I don't know what to say. I'm sorry. I didn't want to hurt you. And I certainly didn't want what happened last night. For God's sake. Someone's got to believe that. It was an accident. Maybe I could have stopped it. I don't have a clue. But it happened. And it happened to me, too. Not just you. You're sorry. I believe you. Now please believe me, too. I've never hurt anyone or anything in my life. I protest against war. I work against poverty. I do everything I can so nobody will be unhappy. I *couldn't* hurt anybody. Except by accident. (*Almost weeping*) For God's sake. Please believe. (*Pauses*) Okay. I guess that's all. You can go, if you want.

JOANNA Oh, damn it. I'm so confused. I don't know what to believe.

ZUCKERMAN (*Moving the chair to center stage*) Please sit down. (*He reaches for her hand. She pulls back violently*)

JOANNA (*Overreacts violently*) Don't you touch me! Oh, you would touch me!

ZUCKERMAN   Look, Miss Dibble, I don't want to touch you.
I just want you to sit down before you faint or something.
You're terribly tense. I can see that and I feel awful about
the whole thing. Just sit down.

JOANNA   Maybe you'd like to make some tea? Or turn on
the phonograph, so we could dance? The killer is so calm.
So matter-of-fact!

ZUCKERMAN   Don't call me a killer.

JOANNA   And why not?

ZUCKERMAN   Because it's . . . cruel . . . yes, it's definitely
cruel. That's why. I didn't do it on purpose. Supposing
you did it. How would you like me coming around up
your place and calling you a "killer" or a "murderer," or
names like that. You think I'm not upset now?

JOANNA   (*That hurt her*)   You insensitive pig. Oh! How
I hate you.

ZUCKERMAN   Well, I don't hate you.

JOANNA   Why should you hate me?

ZUCKERMAN   You're pretty insensitive too, when you get
right down to it. You lack empathy.

JOANNA   (*That really hurt her*)   Empathy?

ZUCKERMAN   (*He mimes the scene casually*)   Sure. Put
yourself in my shoes. You're driving home, right? It's
late. It's raining like hell. You're not a crazy kid, right?
In fact, you're a nice kid. Almost everybody likes you,
except a couple of guys and they're jerks, okay? You

87

haven't been doing anything special, just riding in the rain. You're alone, okay?

JOANNA All right.

ZUCKERMAN Good. Now picture this. You feel a bump. Not even a thump. Just a little bump. You think it's maybe a flat tire. You stop. And it's Frank Weeks Simpson.

JOANNA Oh, dear God. Is that how it happened?

ZUCKERMAN Yes, that's exactly how it happened.

JOANNA You weren't watching. You weren't studying the road. You were just speeding along, not watching a thing. Practically asleep at the wheel. And you ran Frank down. You didn't even slow down first?

ZUCKERMAN That's not what I said at all!

JOANNA You didn't even touch the brakes!

ZUCKERMAN Wait a minute. Now wait a minute. He slipped. Or tripped. Maybe he skated under the car. Yeah—maybe he skated under intentionally to kill himself, for all I know.

JOANNA (*Goes after him fiercely*) That's a lie and you know it!

ZUCKERMAN I didn't say it was positively true. I just said it was a possibility. You're supposed to be in my shoes.

JOANNA I am in your shoes. I am in your shoes.

ZUCKERMAN   Then how come you don't understand?

JOANNA   I understand that I was supposed to be with
Frank last night, but I was too busy. I understand that
Frank went somewhere by himself. I understand that I
was waiting outside for him for twenty minutes before it
became quite evident that he was not going to pick me
up like we had planned. I went and had a drink for a
couple of hours. I was sitting alone with a sculptor who
was almost a complete stranger when someone walks
right up and announces that Frank was dead. Dead.
(*Spells the word*) D-E-A-D. Dead. That I understand.

ZUCKERMAN (*As he clips another clipping*)   Miss Dibble,
if I could live my life over it never would happen, believe
me. They've taken away my car. They've taken away my
license. Do you think this is what I like?

JOANNA   Pleasure? Like? You're not only a killer, you're a
complete madman!

ZUCKERMAN   Everything I say you twist around.

JOANNA (*Sees the newspapers*)   You're interested enough
to buy all the newspapers, I see.

ZUCKERMAN (*Nervously*)   Yeah. Sure. I always buy papers. What the hell. I mean, I'm an English major.

JOANNA (*Sees the scrapbook*)   Oh, my God! A scrapbook.
You're making a scrapbook.

ZUCKERMAN   That's no scrapbook!

JOANNA   Yes it is!

ZUCKERMAN You can't just come running in here and invade my privacy.

JOANNA Oh, dear God. A scrapbook.

ZUCKERMAN That is not a scrapbook.

JOANNA You're collecting things to show your grandchildren. You're enjoying this, killer. Murderer. Assassin.

ZUCKERMAN Give me my scrapbook.
  (*He reaches for it*)

JOANNA Every word of it that's in print, you have. You're making a collection. How many other people are you planning to run over? Look at all these blank pages. How are you going to fill them up?

ZUCKERMAN Jesus, that's not fair!

JOANNA Fair! Fair! Get into my shoes. Go ahead. Get into my shoes.

ZUCKERMAN That's ridiculous!

JOANNA Ridiculous? I got into your shoes.

ZUCKERMAN All right.

JOANNA Yesterday. I was a whole person. A total being. I had my work. I had my man. I had my mind. I had my *love*. Do you know what love is?

ZUCKERMAN Well, yeah. Sort of, I've been in love.

JOANNA With who?

ZUCKERMAN   Oh, lots of times. I'm always in love with somebody. There was Marylin. That was love. Nothing too big, but it sure was love. Of course, right now I'm sort of between things. But I've been around. Yes, sir. I've been around plenty. Love.

JOANNA (*Cuts him off like Zorro with*)   I said LOVE!

ZUCKERMAN   Yeah. Well. I heard you. Love.

JOANNA   Love. Communication between two people. Truth. Beauty. Total commitment. Poetry. *Hands on my breasts*. Trees. Flowers.

ZUCKERMAN (*Stares incredulously in open fascination, peppered with his interpretation of what she is free associating, i.e., his sexual fantasy begins*)   Hands on your breasts?

JOANNA   Love. Real love. Communication between two very real souls. Sensibilities that mesh into one. Bodies that join in love. Love. Simplicity. Simplicity like candy and fruit. Candy and fruit. Two artists living together. Totally. Like Sartre and Simone de Bou . . . de Bou—the name like Jackie Kennedy's. Do you understand at all? Do you understand any bit of what I'm saying?

ZUCKERMAN   Sure I do. Sure. Love. Real love. Like Sartre and Jackie Kennedy. (*Not wanting the fantasy to end. He moves closer*) Tell me more about you and him.

JOANNA   We met. It was in the fall. School had just begun. Frank was tall, you know.

ZUCKERMAN   About my height.

91

JOANNA   A little taller.

ZUCKERMAN   Not too much, though.

JOANNA   He was a thinker. A scholar. He was a Math major, but *potentially* a great artist. We met at a party. Frank was at the party. He was the tallest person there.

ZUCKERMAN   There must have been a lot of short people, 'cause I'm no giant and he was not that much taller than me.

JOANNA   He asked me to go to the mountains with him.

ZUCKERMAN   What mountains?

JOANNA   He had a cabin. In New Hampshire. A hunting lodge.

ZUCKERMAN   Did you go?

JOANNA   He told me about his hunting lodge. How the winters were. About the animals. His eyes were soft. Frank loved animals.

ZUCKERMAN   I like animals. I had a dog once. (*Remembering*) Shit.

JOANNA   What's the matter?

ZUCKERMAN   I had a dog and I killed him by accident.

JOANNA   You killed your dog?

ZUCKERMAN   Why didn't I think of that before? I killed my dog. I ran over him. I had him since I was a kid, too. One night I drove into the driveway and he ran right under the car. He was dead, too.

JOANNA   You killed him with your car?

ZUCKERMAN   I ran right over him. I didn't even see him. (*Pauses*) I've got a knack for this kind of thing. Why didn't I remember?

JOANNA   What else have you killed?

ZUCKERMAN   My own dog. He was a great dog, too. Right over him with my car. First the front wheels. Then the back wheels. He was squashed. How could I forget a thing like that?

JOANNA (*Dead center, straight front*)   We finally went up to his cabin.

ZUCKERMAN (*Confused*)   What cabin?

JOANNA   Frank's cabin. In the mountains.

ZUCKERMAN   You went up there, huh?

JOANNA   It was like a dream. Just Frank and me and the mountains. As far as you could see there was just trees and sky. Green and blue.

ZUCKERMAN   What was the cabin like?

JOANNA (*Elephant tears*)   Split logs. Frank built it with his father. Split logs. Trees that they had taken down together. It was a beautiful place.

ZUCKERMAN   Did they all live there?

JOANNA Who?

ZUCKERMAN Frank's family. His father.

JOANNA No. It was their hunting lodge. No heat or water or anything. Just pure. We burned things to keep warm. We made love . . . and hot chocolate.

ZUCKERMAN Did you go up there often?

JOANNA Very often.

ZUCKERMAN (*Simply, like a pal*) I'd love to go up there sometime. I've never really been up in the mountains like that. Oh, I've never been . . . you know.

JOANNA Not many people have.

ZUCKERMAN You want some hot chocolate? I've got hot chocolate.

JOANNA No. Not now. Not so soon. It wouldn't be right.

ZUCKERMAN (*Walks to the table*) Wheat thin?

JOANNA No, thank you. I'm stuffed.

ZUCKERMAN Want some rosé? (*Starts for the kitchen*) Please stay. I mean, don't go away. I mean, keep talking. I can hear you. (*Calling*) I can hear you.

JOANNA How long have you lived here?
(*She inspects the flat again*)

ZUCKERMAN What?

94

JOANNA (*Walks to his chessboard and "jumps" five black men as in checkers*)   How long have you lived here?

ZUCKERMAN   Oh, about six months. Since school began. I used to have a roommate but he . . . (*A crash sounds in the kitchen*) Christ! (*Pokes his head into the room*) I spilled the wine. (*Reenters; to the world*) He was named Charles.

JOANNA   Who?

ZUCKERMAN   My dog. He had a funny little tail. It got cut off in the screen door. There are people who bite dogs' tails off for a living, you know that?

JOANNA   They bite dogs' tails?

ZUCKERMAN (*Reconsiders*)   That's probably not true. (*Pauses*) I remember once he licked my father's face when he was asleep in the hammock. When I was little I used to hide cookies behind my back and offer Charles a little bit. He used to come behind me and eat the big piece and I'd be left with the little piece. (*Pauses*) And I ran him right over with my car. Right over. How the hell did I forget *that?*

JOANNA   Have you ever thought of getting another dog? You can get dogs for nothing at the rescue-league place.

ZUCKERMAN   I turned the car into the driveway and the stupid Goddamned dog came running up with his tongue hanging out.
    (*He mimics the dog*)

JOANNA (*Dead center again*)   Do you live here alone?

ZUCKERMAN   Yeah.

JOANNA   Don't you have a roommate?

ZUCKERMAN   He flunked out. I'm looking for a roommate, but everybody seems to be settled in. You know what I mean? I ran an ad, but nobody answered. I'll probably get one next semester.

JOANNA   Why don't you live in a dorm?

ZUCKERMAN (*Enters with a tray of beer, wheat thins, wine, olives, etc.*)   Here.

JOANNA   Oh, my goodness.

ZUCKERMAN   You're probably hungry.

JOANNA   I adore olives.

ZUCKERMAN   Go on. Take some. That's what it's there for. Go on.

JOANNA (*Taking some*)   Thank you. Umm, it's good.

ZUCKERMAN   Rosé? Or Heinekens? Or I've got some warm soda water if you'd like.

JOANNA   Heineken's fine.

ZUCKERMAN   Me, too. I like beer a lot. I don't drink too much. Don't get me wrong. But I like to relax with a good foreign beer.

JOANNA   Why don't you live in a dorm?

ZUCKERMAN   I like to be alone. The dorms are stupid.

JOANNA   I thought there was a rule about apartments.

ZUCKERMAN   That's just for out-of-staters. It's very complex. I'm a native. I told them that I live at home. It's okay.

JOANNA   Don't your folks care?

ZUCKERMAN   Naw. They don't care. I pay for this place myself. Why should they care?

JOANNA   Do you work?

ZUCKERMAN   Sure. I load meat.

JOANNA   You load meat?

ZUCKERMAN   My uncle owns a meat market. It's a stupid job.

JOANNA   Meat. I adore meat. It's so basic.

ZUCKERMAN   You wouldn't "adore" it, if you had to handle it every day.

JOANNA   I think it's very beautiful that you handle meat.

ZUCKERMAN   Beautiful? You don't understand. I have to mop the trucks. Trim up lamb chops. Run cheap meat up and in the thing that makes hamburg. What's so beautiful about that?

JOANNA   Meat. Don't you understand?/Meat is even more basic than bread or wine. It's the essence of life. It's terribly symbolic.

97

ZUCKERMAN   I never really thought of it that way.

JOANNA   It's absolutely primitive.

ZUCKERMAN   I guess you just don't think of it that way when it's your stupid uncle's meat in your stupid uncle's meat market.

JOANNA   I think it's really beautiful that you don't work in a shoe store or something. You handle meat.

ZUCKERMAN   (*Realizing he's got a good thing going*) Well, some people are cut out for shoes. I'm just cut out for meat. You know what I mean?

JOANNA   Do you make a lot of money?

ZUCKERMAN   They pay seven-fifty a morning. Oh, yeah. The trucks come in with the meat every morning at five o'clock. They need people to carry the meat in off the trucks. It's wild. (*Now begins the fantasy; the seduction is on*) You take a hook and stand with your back to the truck. Then the guy drops a whole side of beef onto your hook. You walk it into the door and kind of lift up with your back. There's a chain going around with a whole batch of hooks and you wait until one of the hooks grabs ahold of your meat. Then you go out and get another one. (*Pauses, dreaming up a decent climax for his lie*) You follow me?

JOANNA   You do this every day?

ZUCKERMAN   Sure. Every day. Seven days a week. There's nothing to it. I get back here around six and sack out for a couple of hours. They don't take out any income tax or nothing. I clear fifty-two-fifty a week. Almost two-fifty a month. That pays tuition, rent, food, the works. (*Strutting now*) 'Course, I get a scholarship. But the meat pays for everything else.

JOANNA   Wally, you have certain *potential* qualities that are really . . . unique. What's your major?

ZUCKERMAN   Lit. That's how I got to see you in the lesbian thing. We all went. The whole class. You were really terrific.

JOANNA   What's your minor?

ZUCKERMAN   Ed. My art-history ed. class all went to the Common. That's how I saw your paintings. That's some accident—coincidence. (*Pause*) Lit. major, ed. minor.

JOANNA   What do you write?

132468

ZUCKERMAN   I don't. I'm going to teach.

JOANNA   Where?

ZUCKERMAN   Back home. In the high school. In Wakefield.

JOANNA   Have you ever tried writing?

ZUCKERMAN   Ten thousand poems for Creative Poetry 201. Nothing any good, though.

JOANNA   I'd love to read some of your work.

ZUCKERMAN   Really? I'll get them if you'd like.

JOANNA   What time is it?

ZUCKERMAN   Quarter to three. It's early. Have you got a date? (*Realizes what this means*) Wow! I'm sorry, Joanna.

JOANNA   I know. I know. (*Sucks in her breath*) Poetry?

ZUCKERMAN   They're not much, really.

JOANNA   I don't want to put you to any trouble.

ZUCKERMAN   Oh. It's no trouble. None at all. I've got them right over here in the thing. (*Runs to the footlocker and pulls out a sheaf of papers*) See? I never read them to anyone. They're really kind of stupid.

JOANNA   I'd love to read them.

ZUCKERMAN   Here. I'll read one to you.

JOANNA   No. Let me read. I can never understand poetry unless I read it aloud.

ZUCKERMAN   I'll read it *slowly*.

JOANNA   No. Really. You don't understand. Let me read it.

ZUCKERMAN   How about if I read the first one and you read the next one?

JOANNA   No. Please. Let me read.

ZUCKERMAN   Okay. Here. This one's . . . (*Scans the papers*) Naw. That's stupid. (*Finds one he likes*) Here. Here's one. You might like it. It's sort of "yogi."

JOANNA (*Takes the paper and reads*) "Very quiet; cleansed of any passion, the true yogi knows that Brahman is his highest ecstasy." That's lovely. It's so familiar.

ZUCKERMAN Yeah. I based it on something. Actually, it's not completely mine. I sort of paraphrased a thing.

JOANNA It's just lovely. (*Walks and reads with gestures*) "His heart is with Brahman, his eye in all things sees only Brahman, equally present, in every creature and all creation." That's really good. I really like it. What's Brahman?

ZUCKERMAN Well, you know. Brahman is sort of a thing . . . You know. From the swami.

JOANNA Like Atman?

ZUCKERMAN Sure That's right. Like Atman. You know Atman, too, huh? (*Pauses*) What's Atman?

JOANNA Atman is like tranquillity.

ZUCKERMAN So's Brahman. Like tranquillity. (*Changes the subject*) That's a nice word, tranquillity.

JOANNA Tranquillity.

ZUCKERMAN I mean, it's one of those words that sounds like it means.

JOANNA Tranquillity. (*Experiments with the sounds*) Tran. Quill. It. Tee. Tranquillity.

ZUCKERMAN You know what the most beautiful two

words are in the whole English language? You know what?

JOANNA (*Plays the sound*) The most beautiful.

ZUCKERMAN Listen. (*Mouths the words carefully*) Cellar door. Cellar door. Isn't that something? Cellar door.

JOANNA (*Doesn't know what the hell he's talking about*) It sounds so French.

ZUCKERMAN That's right. Cellar door. Name two other words more beautiful. Go on, try. You just can't. Cellar door. (*Excited again*) Hey. You want to hear a great story? I mean a *great* story. It happened back home. I used to pass a gourmet shop on my way to Boston. When I came into my uncle's to work on Sunday. I was just a kid then. I used to come in every Sunday from Wakefield. On the bus. Anyway. There was this gourmet shop. German. They sold pastries and stuff to make your own pastries. Anyway. They had this terrific sign in their window for years advertising dough for strudel. Huge sign. Strudel dough. It was up for years. I used to pass it every Sunday. And I used to think about all those people who had to keep staring at it every day. They never ever changed the sign. I mean, it just *hung* there, taped to the window, getting old and sort of yellow and terrible. Strudel dough. Get it? So one day, I got off the bus near the pastry shop; and I took a magic marker and wrote "strudel dee" right under strudel dough. Isn't that beautiful? (*She's been laughing, but goes deadpan. He's laughing*) Strudel dough. Strudel dee. Can you imagine what all those poor people said when they saw it? After all those years of passing that sign, all of a sudden it's funny. Strudel dough. Strudel dee. You think that's funny, don't you?

JOANNA (*Seriously, intensely*) You'll be a marvelous writer.

ZUCKERMAN You think so?

JOANNA You love words, don't you?

ZUCKERMAN (*Puzzled*) What do you mean?

JOANNA Words. Word sounds. Like strudel dough—strudel dee—cellar door. You're right. I can't think of a more beautiful word. It's silly, yet you're absolutely right. Cellar door. Cellar door.
(*She still doesn't know*)

ZUCKERMAN You're right about their sounding French. Wanna read some more poems?

JOANNA (*Plays the word sounds*) More poems.

ZUCKERMAN Do you know Zen questions?

JOANNA (*Again*) Zen questions.

ZUCKERMAN (*Really excited now*) Yeah. Zen questions. Like, if you were hanging by your teeth from the limb of a tree over a cliff and there were jagged rocks below, and your hands were tied. Get it? Then some guy shows up at the bottom of the tree and asks, "What is Zen?" What would you answer?

JOANNA (*Waits, considering*) That's beautiful.

ZUCKERMAN   Yeah. I've got this place all fixed up for Zen.

JOANNA   How?
   (ZUCKERMAN *begins to go into a series of Zen exercises as* JOANNA *finds his sheaf of poems and begins to sketch him as he talks. He snaps from his pose to pose, demonstrating*)

ZUCKERMAN   There are rules. You can't just meditate *anywhere*. For beginners, you need a clean quiet place with a comfortable temperature. I'm getting a Puritron.

JOANNA   Puritron.

ZUCKERMAN   Your place should be well ventilated. No problem there. There are things about your body. A true Zen keeps a certain kind of physical condition. Exercises. They hurt at first, but you get used to them. No associations with men of fame or those who like to argue or those who enjoy competitive sports. "If you can't beat 'em, Zen-out," that's what I always say. And no view that distracts the mind. Usually I don't have that kind of problem. (*Giggles at his joke. Checks* JOANNA *for a laugh. Nothing. Goes on*) That's all I can remember. I've got the rules written down. You're drawing on them. (*She looks up*) That's okay. It's just an old blue book. If you ever want to cheat, buy blank blue books and write lists out in the back with the same pen you bring into the test. When they pass out the blue books, ask for two. Then switch one quick, while they're still passing out. I don't cheat much. Just when the tests are dumb.

JOANNA   That's brilliant.

ZUCKERMAN   You're the first person I've ever told, you know that? I'll bet I could tell anybody else and the whole city would be buying blue books tomorrow. It's incredible that nobody ever thought of that before, isn't it? You want something? Food? A pillow? Do you want anything at all?

JOANNA You're very attentive. Very loving. Very gentle. You're almost virginal. You know that?

ZUCKERMAN (*Struck down, he tries to be cool*) Virginal? Virginal? Listen. I've been in love plenty. Real love. Like you say. Sensibilities and stuff like Sartre. If you'll pardon my saying it, I've had my hands on plenty of breasts. You think I'm just a kid, right? Well, let me tell you a little bit of news, Miss Dibble, I've been around. And I mean *around*. I've got a list as long as your hair. Rachael. Marylin. Marsha. Alice. Bonnie. (*Thinks*) Did I say Marylin? Yeah. Marylin. And Bonnie. Maybe I haven't slept around all over the place, but I've been pretty close. Pretty close. There was Marylin. Yes, sir. There certainly was. (*Now he's shaken. He pauses— back to the papers. Reading*) Here's one I never understood. "Do not waste your time writing poems and essays about Zen."

JOANNA Are you sure that's right?

ZUCKERMAN I copied it right out of the book. (*As he explains the "message," she does a "take," saying "oh." He knows now*) I mean, the message of the man hanging by his teeth is not to open your mouth, right? And they tell you not to argue. Maybe they lost something in the translation. Mah-nish-ta-noh. Ha li-loh ha-zeh. Mikol ha-lay-los.

JOANNA Do you translate?

ZUCKERMAN (*Very proud, very cool*) Oh, a little bit.

JOANNA You're really a thinker, aren't you?

ZUCKERMAN (*Honestly*) I never really have anybody to talk to. Those guys down at the market laugh at me.

JOANNA What do they know?

ZUCKERMAN (*Classic paranoia*) Oh, I don't put them down. I mean, they're REAL people. You know what I mean? They don't go to school or anything. They're definitely real. It's sort of crazy, but sometimes I think I'm more comfortable with them than with anyone else. It's crazy, especially since they hate me. They don't even talk to me. Not for two years. They really hate me.

JOANNA No. I understand. Just being with kids all the time. It drives me crazy. I envy you.

ZUCKERMAN You envy *me?*

JOANNA Sure. I'd love to carry meat like you do. I have to take money from home, you know what I mean?

ZUCKERMAN You couldn't carry meat.

JOANNA That's the point. There's so little a woman can do. Alone, I mean. Artists belong together. Don't you think so? I can paint all right. But I can't make a living from it. Not yet, anyway. All that there's for me is some silly job selling dresses or something. I'd like to be able to do some real work. To meet some real people. Like you do. Every day. Not just once in a while. (*Pauses for the greatest line ever written*) Could I come down to the market with you?

ZUCKERMAN   Would you like to?

JOANNA   I'd adore it. Oh, could I?

ZUCKERMAN   Sure. You could come down whenever you like. It's not too exciting, though. But we could walk around the waterfront. Have you ever walked around the waterfront?

JOANNA   A few times.

ZUCKERMAN   You ought to walk around down there at five-fifteen every morning. That's when it's great. At dawn. I go there all the time, when we break from the meat. I go off by myself. You've got to see it. The men like to break alone, so I walk over to the harbor. When we break from the meat.

JOANNA   I'd love to.

ZUCKERMAN   There are fishing boats. And real fishermen. Honest to God. Real fishermen. They make their living fishing. You'd never think there were any real fishermen left, would you?

JOANNA   Not around here.

ZUCKERMAN   (*On the verge of total ecstasy*) There are. Hundreds of them. They work the docks. They're great. Yellow slickers. Big boots. Paper hats. (*Pauses*) Oh, yeah. I act kind of different with them though. I have to be sort of one of them.

JOANNA   What do you do?

ZUCKERMAN   First off, you have to make a hat out of newspaper. To keep the blood and junk out of your hair.

(*Demonstrates by taking the newspaper that was de-livered before* JOANNA's *entrance. He unfolds the first section and chooses the right shape and size, then begins to fold his hat*) See. This is a big status thing. I mean, the easiest way to spot a phony is by his paper hat. It took me weeks to figure out how the hell to make this stupid thing. (*He finishes and puts the newspaper hat on his head*)

JOANNA   Ohh.

ZUCKERMAN   There you are. Nice, huh? You've got to ad-mit, even after seven years of schlepping meat, I've got clean hair. Right? There's more to it.

JOANNA   What?

ZUCKERMAN   More things you have to do to fit in.

JOANNA   More hats?

ZUCKERMAN   Hell no. That turned out to be the easiest part of it. You've got to walk tough.

JOANNA   Walk tough?

ZUCKERMAN   (*Demonstrates, strutting like crazy*)   See? I walk tough. And I spit a lot. That's really important. You have to spit a lot. They spit all the time. And you have to talk dirty. You might not like that.

JOANNA (*Jumps up and runs to him, giggling*)   I'd love it. You're wrong. I'd love it.
     (*They embrace, at first, from* JOANNA's *enthusiasm. Then they embrace, sensing that it's happened.*

*They hold each other childishly. Then they kiss, a
long delicious kiss. They break apart as* ZUCKERMAN
holds JOANNA *at arm's length*)

ZUCKERMAN   Joanna. I love you. I love you.

JOANNA   Oh, Wally.

ZUCKERMAN   Ever since the play I've loved you. You know
that?

JOANNA   Oh, Wally. My knees are all rubbery. I feel funny
all over. (*They kiss again. Their hands search each
other's body. Then they embrace, still kissing, as* ZUCKER-
MAN *bends her backwards, kissing her as passionately
as he can. They break apart.* JOANNA *holds his face in
her hands. He stares into her eyes, helpless*) I love you,
Wally. I know I love you. Your face. Your funny hat.
(*Suddenly she spies her picture on his hat*) Oh, my God!
He used that picture.

ZUCKERMAN   Huh? What picture?

JOANNA   It's the paper. The story. The picture. He used a
horrible picture.

ZUCKERMAN   That was my high school picture.

JOANNA   No, the one of me.

ZUCKERMAN   (*Pulling the hat from his head, he tears it
apart, searching frantically*)   What one of you?

JOANNA   (*Points it out*)   How could he? I look ridiculous.

ZUCKERMAN   Where'd they get that? What's this? How'd
they get yours?

JOANNA   A reporter came around last night. He took pictures from me.

ZUCKERMAN (*Pulls the paper back from her. Reading*) "Joanna Dibble. Twenty-one-year-old artist." Artist? You're a student. You go to school. What's this crap?

JOANNA   You're an artist.

ZUCKERMAN   I am not.

JOANNA   He came around last night. We talked for a long time and I was upset. He asked personal questions. You know.

ZUCKERMAN (*Reading*)   "Our love was pure." Pure? Holy Jesus! I'll say he asked personal questions!

JOANNA   I was upset, Wally. I never would have given him that picture if I was thinking clearly.

ZUCKERMAN   "We went to his cabin." Jumping Jesus. Jumping Jesus Christ! Why did you do this?

JOANNA   I was all calmed down. Now you're making it all awful again. Don't do this, Wally. Don't do this. I'm not going to let you get me going again. I'm staying calm.

ZUCKERMAN   "We went to his cabin!" How could you say that? How could you let that get into the papers? Tell me! What prompted you to tell him? To tell anybody?

JOANNA (*Pulls it away*)   I was very upset. (*They spread it on the floor*) "Heartbroken, tearful, full of contempt. She wept for twenty minutes before she could speak. And when she spoke, her words sobbed."

110

ZUCKERMAN Who the hell wrote this?

JOANNA The reporter, silly.

ZUCKERMAN He came last night?

JOANNA This morning.

ZUCKERMAN You said last night.

JOANNA I meant this morning. What difference does it make?

ZUCKERMAN (*Cuckolded*) Nobody came *here* this morning.

JOANNA Your picture's here.

ZUCKERMAN That's the same one. Look how little it is.

JOANNA They had the big one this morning.

ZUCKERMAN Why didn't you tell me about this?

JOANNA Why?

ZUCKERMAN "And when she spoke, her words sobbed." That's the most ridiculous thing I ever read. "Sobbed."

JOANNA I was very upset.

ZUCKERMAN "New wrinkle"? You're a "new wrinkle." What does that mean?

JOANNA That's newspaper talk.

ZUCKERMAN Newspaper talk? What kind of talk is that?

JOANNA I was the fiancée. Human interest.

ZUCKERMAN Human interest! You weren't anywhere near the accident. What the hell is all of this about?

JOANNA It's only a story. He said that my love was a "new wrinkle."

ZUCKERMAN But how did he *know* about you? Who told him?

JOANNA I called the papers.

ZUCKERMAN You *what?*

JOANNA I was engaged to be married.

ZUCKERMAN I know. You were engaged to be married. Swell.

JOANNA Well, that's enough reason. Isn't it?

ZUCKERMAN Am I crazy or are you crazy? Is this a *game?*

JOANNA It's just news. Wally, you know how I feel about you.

ZUCKERMAN How you feel about *me?* This whole thing's about *you.* How the hell did this happen?

JOANNA Wally, a reporter came to the dorm. He asked me questions about the way I felt. And I answered him. It's news. News. *I* was *engaged* to him. They wanted my statement. Why are you so upset?

112

ZUCKERMAN What about *my* statement? Doesn't the count? There was a witness. An honest-to-God witness. A judge yet. I didn't even get a second statement. This is terrible.

JOANNA Look at that horrible picture.

ZUCKERMAN (*To the world*) Jesus. She doesn't like her picture. Two inches of my school picture and you're upset. Look at the pimples. YOU'RE upset. That's the most ridiculous thing I ever heard of.

JOANNA But we both have our pictures in. Look, Wally, our pictures are together. Sort of side by side.
   (*Dialogue dissolves—overlays as they tear through the newspapers*)

ZUCKERMAN I had a suspicion that something was wrong. I felt it. I never expected anything like this! Never. You knifed me, that's what. Wally Zuckerman gets knifed again.

JOANNA I never should have let him use that picture. Aren't they supposed to get a release? Can they just go ahead and print whatever they want? That's such a ridiculous picture.

ZUCKERMAN I just can't understand it. Not one new picture.

JOANNA He didn't bring a photographer. That's probably why. There wasn't time. They *had* to use old pictures.

ZUCKERMAN You knew it all along. You knew it. You wanted to take this away from me. That's why you came here. To take this from me.

113

JOANNA   That's not true. That's not true. I don't tell lies. That's not true.

ZUCKERMAN (*Menacingly*)   Lies? True? I don't believe this. I don't believe it! You came here to steal. Steal. Steal it from me. Isn't that right. Huh. Isn't that right? I've got to be the dumbest dummy ever made. (*Sees her drawing of him*) What are you going to call that picture? "Dumb-Dumb"?

JOANNA   He got pictures. He got pictures of the two of us. Old pictures. But pictures of the two of us. Together almost.

ZUCKERMAN   I sat in the police station last night. Not you. I did.

JOANNA   I was engaged to him.

ZUCKERMAN (*Tears her drawing to bits and throws it about his room. He rips newsclippings from his bulletin board and tears them as well. This is FURY*)   I carry the God-damned meat. Up with the meat. Down with the meat.

JOANNA   I loved him.

ZUCKERMAN   I walk along that stupid waterfront. Staring at nothing at all!

JOANNA   I was part of his life.

ZUCKERMAN   I sit in the rooms. I cram my head fat with nothing at all. Why? Don't you understand? Something finally happened. What in hell do you think I've been waiting for? Now it's gone. It's gone. It's nothing.

JOANNA   You have a life, Wally. You and I. You have your Work. I have my Work.

ZUCKERMAN   You carry the meat tomorrow. You carry the meat. I'll paint trash cans. (*Mimes as well*) I'll run around playing lesbians. I don't know what I'll do. I'll probably lose my license over this for sure. Why?

JOANNA   You love me.

ZUCKERMAN   Love you? That's more baloney. I don't even know you. Who are you, anyway?

JOANNA   It's me, Joanna Dibble. Wally, what's happened?

ZUCKERMAN   Wallace Zuckerman. A schmucky name like that. I was born with a silver knife in my back. How many chances do you think I'll get in my life? Just how many do you think I'll ever get?

JOANNA   How many fiancés will I lose?

ZUCKERMAN   A million. You'll be a widow ten times over. You'll have plenty of chances and you know it. (*Walks to the scrapbook*) Three dollars blown on this. One hundred and seventeen globs of hamburger up and in. This is mine. Not yours. Not a bit of it. You're nothing. Nothing. Now there's complications. Implications. New faces. New story. New wrinkles. Where is Wally? Huh? Where is Wally in all of this? Where am I?

JOANNA   Wally. You love me. You love me, damn it.

ZUCKERMAN   (*Slaps her fiercely across the face. She steps back and touches her cheek. She slaps him. He slaps her.*

Once more. Another exchange of blows. She falls) Oh, Jesus.

JOANNA Oh, Wally.
(*She walks to him and they kiss passionately*)

ZUCKERMAN (*Breaks, after a long kiss*) Screw it. It's only a story, that's all. It's just a story.
(*They settle to the floor together.* JOANNA *crawls to* ZUCKERMAN. *He cradles her in his lap. She speaks quietly, as in a dream*)

JOANNA Tell me how it's going to be, Wally. He was sweet. But not nearly as sweet as you. Not nearly as gentle. Will you always be gentle, Wally?
(*He's caught pulling back the bedspread*)

ZUCKERMAN (*The lights begin to fade, slowly, until they are pinspotted alone*) Tomorrow we'll get up just before dawn. We'll walk to the waterfront.

JOANNA I'd like that. But I'd like to take walks with you when the sun is orange, beside the moon.

ZUCKERMAN We'll watch the sun break at dawn. Over the harbor. It's pretty there. The fishermen. They're *real* people.

JOANNA You know when that is, Wally? That's the time I love best of all. At the end of the day and the beginning of the night. The sun is orange and the moon is just a trace of yellow.

ZUCKERMAN No, at dawn. I'll load the meat and you can watch me.

116

JOANNA   That's when I know there are two other places
. . . two other places.

ZUCKERMAN   When I'm through, we can walk back to the
harbor. There's a ship I want you to see. It's really a tug-
boat. It's called the *Sugar Plum*.

JOANNA (*Pulls him into an embrace*)   That's right. Candy
and fruit. Candy and fruit. That's all I'm looking for.
That's all.

ZUCKERMAN   No, it's called the *Sugar Plum* . . . It's called
the *Sugar Plum*.

JOANNA   That's all I'm looking for. That's all.

ZUCKERMAN   I think it's called the *Sugar Plum*.

(*The lights switch to black. Curtain*)

the indian
wants /
the bronx

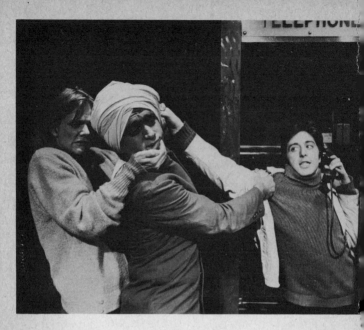

The Indian Wants the Bronx: Matthew Cowles as JOEY;
John Cazale (also winner of the 1968 OBIE Award for
Distinguished Performance in *The Indian Wants the
Bronx*) as GUPTA; Al Pacino (winner of the 1968 OBIE
Award for Best Actor of the Year in *The Indian Wants
the Bronx*) as MURPH.

THE INDIAN WANTS THE BRONX *was presented by Ruth Newton Productions on January 17, 1968, at the Astor Place Theatre, New York City, with the following cast:*

(In order of appearance)

GUPTA, an East Indian   John Cazale
MURPH   Al Pacino
JOEY   Matthew Cowles

Directed by James Hammerstein

Prior to its New York opening, THE INDIAN WANTS THE BRONX *was presented as a work-in-progress at The Loft Workshop, New York; The Eugene O'Neill Memorial Theatre Foundation, Connecticut; Canoe Place Cabaret Theatre, New York; and The Act IV Café Theatre, Massachusetts.*

Place: A bus stop on upper Fifth
Avenue in New York City.

Time: A chilly September's night.

There is no crime greater,
more worthy of punishment,
than being strange and
frightened among the strange
and frightened . . . except
assimilation to the end of
becoming strange and
frightened, but apart from
one's own real self.

*As the curtains open the
lights fade up, revealing* GUPTA, *an East Indian. He is
standing alone, right of center stage, near a bus stop sign.
An outdoor telephone booth is to his left; several city-
owned litter baskets are to his right.*

GUPTA *is in his early fifties. Although he is swarthy in
complexion, he is anything but sinister. He is, in fact, meek
and visibly frightened by the city.*

*He is dressed in traditional East Indian garb, appropri-
ately for mid-September.*

As GUPTA *strains to look for a bus on the horizon, the
voices of two boys can be heard in the distance, singing.
They sing a rock-'n'-roll song, flatly, trying to harmonize.*

FIRST BOY
 I walk the lonely streets at night,
 A 'lookin' for your door,
 I look and look and look and look,
 But, baby, you don't care.
 Baby, you don't care.
 Baby, no one cares.

SECOND BOY (*Interrupting*)   Wait a minute, Joey. I'll take
 the harmony. Listen. (*Singing*)
 But, baby, you don't care.
 Baby, you don't care.
 Baby, no one cares.

(*Confident that he has fully captured the correct harmony, boasting*) See? I've got a knack for harmony. You take the low part.

BOYS (*Singing together*)
I walk . . . the lonely, lonely street . . .
A 'listenin' for your heartbeat,
Listening for your love.
But, baby, you don't care.
Baby, you don't care.
Baby, no one cares.
   (*They appear on stage.* FIRST BOY *is* JOEY. SECOND BOY *is* MURPH. JOEY *is slight, baby-faced, in his early twenties.* MURPH *is stronger, long-haired, the same age*)

MURPH (*Singing*)
The lonely, lonely streets, called out for lovin,'
But there was no one to love . . .
'Cause, baby, you don't care . . .

JOEY (*Joins in the singing*)
Baby, you don't care . . .

JOEY AND MURPHY (*Singing together*)
Baby, you don't care.
Baby, you don't care.
Baby, no one cares.
Baby, no one cares.

MURPH (*Calls out into the audience, to the back row: across to the row of apartment houses opposite the park*)   Hey, Pussyface! Can you hear your babies singing? Pussyface. We're calling you.

JOEY (*Joins in*) Pussyface. Your babies are serenading your loveliness.
(*They laugh*)

MURPH Baby, no one cares.

MURPH AND JOEY (*Singing together*)
Baby, no one cares.
Baby, no one cares.

MURPH (*Screams*) Pussyface, you don't care, you God-damned idiot! (*Notices* THE INDIAN) Hey. Look at the Turk.
(JOEY *stares at* THE INDIAN *for a moment, then replies*)

JOEY Just another pretty face. Besides. That's no Turk. It's an Indian.

MURPH (*Continues to sing*)
Baby, no one cares.
(*Dances to his song, strutting in* THE INDIAN's *direction. He then turns back to* JOEY *during the completion of his stanza and feigns a boxing match*)
I walk the lonely, lonely streets,
A 'callin' out for loving,
But, baby, you don't give a Christ for
Nothin' . . . not for nothin'.
(*Pretends to swing a punch at* JOEY, *who backs off laughing*) You're nuts. It's a Turk!

JOEY Bet you a ten spot. It's an Indian.

MURPH It's a Turk, schmuck. Look at his fancy hat. Indians don't wear fancy hats. (*Calls across the street, again*) Hey, Pussyface. Joey thinks we got an Indian. (*Back to* JOEY) Give me a cigarette.

JOEY You owe me a pack already, Murphy.

MURPH So I owe you a pack. Give me a cigarette.

JOEY Say "please," maybe?

MURPH Say "I'll bust your squash if you don't give me a cigarette!"

JOEY One butt, one noogie.

MURPH First the butt.

JOEY You're a Jap, Murphy.
(*As* JOEY *extends the pack,* MURPH *grabs it*)

MURPH You lost your chance, baby. (*To the apartment block*) Pussyface! Joey lost his chance!

JOEY We made a deal. A deal's a deal. You're a Jap, Murphy. A rotten Jap. (*To the apartment*) Pussyface, listen to me! Murphy's a rotten Jap and just Japped my whole pack. That's unethical, Pussyface. He owes me noogies, too!

MURPH Now I'll give you twenty noogies, so we'll be even. (*He raps* JOEY *on the arm.* THE INDIAN *looks up as* JOEY *squeals*)

JOEY Hey. The Indian's watching.

MURPH (*Raps* JOEY *sharply again on the arm*) Indian's a Turkie.

JOEY (*Grabs* MURPH's *arm and twists it behind his back*)
Gimme my pack and it's an Indian, right?

MURPH   I'll give you your head in a minute, jerkoff.

JOEY   Indian? Indian? Say, Indian!

MURPH   Turkie? Turkie?

JOEY   Turkie. Okay. Let go.
(MURPH *lets him up and laughs.* JOEY *jumps up and screams*) Indian! (*Runs a few steps*) Indian!

MURPH (*Laughing*)   If your old lady would have you on Thanksgiving you'd know what a turkey was, ya' jerk. (*Hits him on the arm again*) Here's another noogie, Turkie-head!
(THE INDIAN *coughs*)

JOEY   Hey, look. He likes us. Shall I wink?

MURPH   You sexy beast, you'd wink at anything in pants.

JOEY   Come on. Do I look like a Murphy?

MURPH (*Grabs* JOEY *and twists both of his arms*)   Take that back.

JOEY   Aw! ya' bastard. I take it back.

MURPH   You're a Turkie-lover, right?

JOEY   Right.

MURPH   Say it.

JOEY   I'm a Turkie-lover.

MURPH   You're a Turkie-humper, right?

JOEY   *You're* a Turkie-humper.

MURPH   Say, *I'm* a Turkie-humper.

JOEY   That's what I said. You're a Turkie-humper.
(MURPH *twists his arms a bit further*) Oww, ya' dirty
bastard! All right, I'm a Turkie-humper! Now, leggo!
(JOEY *pretends to laugh*)

MURPH   You gonna hug him and kiss him and love him up
like a mother?

JOEY   Whose mother?

MURPH   Your mother. She humps Turkies, right?

JOEY   Owww! All right. Yeah. She humps Turkies. Now
leggo!

MURPH (*Lets go*)   You're free.

JOEY (*Breaks. Changes the game*)   Where's the bus?

MURPH   Up your mother.

JOEY   My old lady's gonna' kill me. It must be late as hell.

MURPH   So why don't you move out?

JOEY   Where to?

MURPH   Maybe we'll get our own place. Yeah. How about
that, Joey?

JOEY   Yeah, sure. I move out on her and she starves. You know that.

MURPH   Let her starve, the Turkie-humper.

JOEY   (*Hits* MURPH *on the arm and laughs*)   That's my mother you're desecrating, you nasty bastard.

MURPH   How do you desecrate a whore? Call her a lady?

JOEY   Why don't you ask *your* mother?

MURPH   (*Hits* JOEY *on the arm*)   Big mouth, huh?

JOEY   Hey! Why don't you pick on som'body your own size, like Turkie, there.

MURPH   Leave Turkie out of this. He's got six elephants in his pocket, probably.

JOEY   (*Laughs at the possibility*)   Hey, Turkie, you got six elephants in your pocket?

MURPH   Hey, shut up, Joey. (*Glances in* THE INDIAN's *direction and* THE INDIAN *glances back*) Shut up.

JOEY   Ask him for a match.

MURPH   You ask him.

JOEY   You got the butts.

MURPH   Naw.

JOEY   Chicken. Want some seeds to chew on?

MURPH   I'll give you somethin' to chew on.

JOEY   Go on, ask him. I ain't never heard an Indian talk
Turkie-talk.

MURPH   He's a Turkie, I told ya'. Any jerk can see that he's
a definite Turk!

JOEY   You're a definite jerk, then. 'Cause I see a definite
Indian!

MURPH   I'll show you.
(*Walks toward* THE INDIAN *slowly, taking a full
minute to cross the stage. He slithers from side to
side and goes through pantomime of looking for
matches*)

JOEY   Hey, Murph. You comin' for dinner? We're havin'
turkey tonight! Hey! Tell your Turkie to bring his elephants.

MURPH   Schmuck! How's he going to fit six elephants in a
rickshaw?

JOEY (*Flatly*)   Four in front. Three in back.
(*He reaches* THE INDIAN)

MURPH   Excuse me. May I borrow a match?

INDIAN (*Speaking in Hindi*)   Mai toom-haree bo-lee nrh-
hee bol sak-tah. Mai tum-hah-ree bah-sha nah-hee sah-
maj-tah.
(*I cannot speak your language. I don't understand.*)

MURPH (*To* JOEY, *does a terrific "take," then speaks, in-
credulous*)   He's got to be kidding.
(JOEY *and* MURPH *laugh*)

134

INDIAN   Moo-jhay mahaf kar-nah mai toom-hah-ree bah-art nah-hee sah-maj sak-tah.
      (*I'm sorry. I don't understand you.*)

MURPH   No speak English, huh? (THE INDIAN *looks at him blankly. Louder*) You can't speak English, huh?
      (THE INDIAN *stares at him, confused by the increase in volume*)

JOEY (*Flatly*)   Son of a bitch. Hey, Murph. Guess what? Your Turkie only speaks Indian.

MURPH (*Moves in closer, examining* THE INDIAN)   Say something in Indian, big mouth.

JOEY (*Holds up his hand*)   How's your teepee? (THE INDIAN *stares at him. He laughs*) See.
      (THE INDIAN *welcomes* JOEY's *laugh and smiles. He takes their hands and "shakes" them*)

MURPH (*Catches on as to why* THE INDIAN *has joined the smile and feigns a stronger smile until they all laugh aloud.* MURPH *cuts off the laughter as he shakes* THE INDIAN's *hand and says*)   You're a fairy, right?

INDIAN (*Smiles harder than before*)   Mai toom-haree bah-at nah-hee sah-maj-tah. Mai ap-nay lah-kay kah gha-r dhoo-nd rah-haw hooh. Oos-nay moo-jhay mil-nah tar pahr nah-jah-nay woh cah-hah hai. Mai oos-kah mah-kan dhoo-nd rah-hah hoon. Oos-kah pah-tah yeh rah-hah k-yah.
      (*I don't understand you. I'm looking for my son's home. We were supposed to meet, but I could not find him. I'm looking for his home. This is his address. Am I headed in the correct direction?*)

135

(THE INDIAN *produces a slip of paper with an address typed on it. And a photograph*)

MURPH Gupta. In the Bronx. Big deal. (*To* THE INDIAN) Indian, right? You an Indian, Indian? (*Shakes his head up and down, smiling.* THE INDIAN *smiles, confused*) He don't know. (*Pauses, studies the picture, smiles*) This picture must be his kid. Looks like you, Joe.

JOEY (*Looks at the picture*) Looks Irish to me. (*He hands the picture to* MURPH)

BOTH Ohhh.

MURPH Yeah. Why'd you rape all those innocent children? (*Pause*) I think he's the wrong kind of Indian. (*To* THE INDIAN) You work in a restaurant? (*Pauses. Speaks with a homosexual's sibilant "s"*) It's such a shame to kill these Indians. They do such superb beaded work.
    (MURPH *shakes his head up and down again, smiling*)

INDIAN (*Follows* MURPH'S *cue*) Mai-nay ap-nay lar-kay koh su-bah say nah-hee day-kha. Toom-hara shah-har bah-hoot hee barah hai.
    (*I haven't seen my son all day. Your city is so big and so busy.*)

JOEY Ask him to show you his elephants.

MURPH You ask. You're the one who speaks Turkie-Indian.

JOEY White man fork with tongue. Right? (THE INDIAN *stares at him blankly*) Naw, he don't understand me.

You ask. You got the right kind of accent. All you for-
eigners understand each other good.

MURPH   You want another noogie?

JOEY   Maybe Turkie wants a noogie or six?

MURPH (*Shaking his head*)   You want a noogie, friend?

INDIAN (*Agrees*)   Moo-jhay mahaf kar-nah. Moo-jay. Yah-
han aye zyah-da sah-may na-hee hoo-ah.
        (*I'm sorry. I haven't been here long.*)

MURPH   Give him his noogie.

JOEY   Naw. He's your friend. You give it to him. That's
what friends are for.

MURPH (*Looks at the paper and photograph, gives them
back*)   Jesus, look at that for a face.

JOEY   Don't make it.

MURPH   Don't make it. Prem Gupta. In the Bronx. Jesus,
this is terrific. The Indian wants the Bronx.

JOEY (*Sits on a trash can*)   He ain't gonna find no Bronx
on this bus.

MURPH   Old Indian, pal. You ain't going to find the Bronx
on this bus, unless they changed commissioners again.
Now I've got a terrific idea for fun and profit.
        (*Pauses*)

INDIAN   K-yah kah-ha toom-nay?
        (*Excuse me?*)

MURPH   Right. Now why don't you come home and meet my mother? Or maybe you'd like to meet Pussyface, huh? (*To* JOEY) Should we bring him over to Pussyface?

JOEY   He don't even know who Pussyface is. You can't just go getting Indians blind dates without giving him a breakdown.

MURPH   Okay, Chief. Here's the breakdown on Pussyface. She's a pig. She lives right over there. See that pretty building? (*Points over the audience to the back row of seats*) That one. The fancy one. That's Pussyface's hideaway. She's our social worker.

JOEY   That's right.

MURPH   Pussyface got assigned to us when ᴡe were tykers, right, Joe?

JOEY   Just little fellers.

MURPH   Pussyface was sent to us by ᴛhe city. To watch over us. And care for us. And love ᴜ ᴛike a mother. Not because she wanted to. Because wᴇ ᴡere bad boys. We stole a car.

JOEY   We stole two cars.

MURPH   We stole two cars. And we knifed a kid.

JOEY   You knifed a kid.

MURPH (*To* JOEY)   Tell it to the judge, Fella!
           (*He takes a pocketknife from his pocket and shows it to* THE INDIAN, *who pulls back in fear*)

JOEY   The Chief thinks you're going to cut him up into a totem pole.

MURPH   Easy, Chief. I've never cut up an Indian in my life.

JOEY   You've never *seen* an Indian in your life.

MURPH   Anyway, you got a choice. My mother—who happens to have a terrific personality. Or Pussyface, our beloved social lady.

JOEY   Where's the bus?

MURPH   It's coming.

JOEY   S. Christmas.

MURPH   Hey. ow Turkie my Christmas card for Pussyface. (*To the* INDIAN) Pussyface gives us fun projects. I had to make Ch 'mas cards last year. (*Back to* JOEY) Go on. Show the C. f the card.
       (JOEY *fishes thro h his wallet, finds a dog-eared photostat, hands it t* INDIAN, *who accepts curiously*)

INDIAN   Yeh k-yah hai?
       (*What is this?*)

MURPH   I made that with my own two cheeks. Tell h. Joe.

JOEY   Stupid, he don't speak English.

MURPH   It don't matter. He's interested, ain't he?

JOEY   You're a fink-jerk.

MURPH   Oooo. I'll give you noogies up the kazzooo. (*Takes the card away from* THE INDIAN *and explains*) This is a Christmas card. I made it! I made it! Get me? Pussyface got us Christmas jobs last year. She got me one with the city. With the war on poverty. I ran the Xerox machine.

JOEY   Jesus. You really are stupid. He don't understand one word you're saying.

MURPH   (*Mimes the entire scene, slowly*)   He's interested, ain't he? That's more than I can say for most of them. (*To* THE INDIAN) Want to know how you can make your own Christmas cards with your simple Xerox 2400? It's easy. Watch. (*He mimes*) First you lock the door to the stat room, so no one can bust in. Then you turn the machine on. Then you set the dial at the number of people you want to send cards to. Thirty, forty.

JOEY   Three or four.

MURPH   Right, fella. Then you take off your pants. And your underpants that's underneath. You sit on the glass. You push the little button. The lights flash. When the picture's developed, you write "Noel" across it! (*Pauses*) That's how you make Christmas cards. (*Waits for a reaction from* THE INDIAN, *then turns back to* JOEY, *dismayed*) He's waiting for the bus.

JOEY   Me too. Jesus. Am I ever late!

MURPH   Tell her to stuff it. You're a big boy now.

JOEY   She gets frightened, that's all. She really don't care how late I come in, as long as I tell her when I'm coming. If I tell her one, and I don't get in until one-thirty, she's purple when I finally get in. (*Pauses*) She's all right. Where's the Goddamned bus, huh? (*Calls across the park*) Pussyface, did you steal the bus, you dirty old whore? Pussyface, I'm calling you! (*Pauses*) She's all right, Murph. Christ, she's my mother. I didn't ask for her. She's all right.

MURPH   Who's all right? That Turkie-humper? (*To* THE INDIAN) His old lady humps Turkies, you know that? (*Smiles, but* THE INDIAN *doesn't respond*) Hey, Turkie's blowin' his cool a little. Least you got somebody waitin'. My old lady wouldn't know if I was gone a year.

JOEY   What? That Turkie-humper?

MURPH (*To* THE INDIAN) Hey! (THE INDIAN *jumps, startled.* MURPH *laughs*) You got any little Indians runnin' around your teepee? No? Yeah? No? No, ya' stupid Indian. Where is the Goddamn bus?

JOEY   Let's walk it.

MURPH   Screw that. A hundred blocks? Besides, we gotta keep this old Turkie company, right? We couldn't let him stand all alone in the big ole city. Some nasty boys might come along and blow him up, right?

JOEY   We can walk it. Let the Indian starve.

MURPH   So walk it, jerk. I'm waiting with the Chief.
          (MURPH *stands next to* THE INDIAN)

JOEY   Come on, we'll grab the subway.

MURPH   Joe, the trains are running crazy now. Anyway, I'm waitin' with my friend the Chief, here. You wanna

141

go, go. (*Murmurs*) Where is it, Chief? Is that it? Here it comes, huh?

JOEY (*Considers it*)   Yeah, we gotta watch out for Turkie.
(JOEY *stands on the other side of* THE INDIAN, *who finally walks slowly back to the bus stop area*)

MURPH   See that, Turkie, little Joe's gonna keep us company. That's nice, huh? (THE INDIAN *looks for the bus*) You know, Joey, this Turk's a pain in my ass. He don't look at me when I talk to him.

JOEY   He oughta look at you when you talk. He oughta be polite.
(*They pass the card in a game.* THE INDIAN *smiles*)

MURPH   I don't think he learned many smarts in Indiana. Any slob knows enough to look when they're being talked to. Huh?

JOEY   This ain't just any slob. This is a definite Turkie-Indian slob.
(*They pass the card behind their backs*)

MURPH   He's one of them commie slobs, probably. War-mongering bastard. (*Flatly*) Pinko here rapes all the little kids.

JOEY   Terrible thing. Too bad we can't give him some smarts. Maybe he could use a couple.
(*The game ends.* JOEY *has the card as in a magic act*)

MURPH   We'll give him plenty of smarts. (*Calling him up-stage*) Want some smarts? Chief?

INDIAN   Bna-ee mai toom-maree bah-at nah-hee sah-maj-
sak-tah. Bus yah-han kis sa-may a-tee haj. K-yah mai
sa-hee BUS STOP par shoon!
(*I can't understand you. Please? When is the bus
due here? Am I at the right station?*)

JOEY   Hey, look. He's talking out of the side of his mouth.
Sure, that's right . . . Hey, Murph. Ain't Indian broads
s'posed to have sideways breezers? Sure.

MURPH   (*Grins*)   You mean chinks, Joey.

JOEY   Naw. Indian broads too. All them foreign broads.
Their breezers are sideways. That's why them foreign
cars have the back seat facing the side, right?

MURPH   Is that right, Turkie? Your broads have horizontal
snatches?

INDIAN   (*Stares at him nervously*)   Mai toom-haree bah-
at nah-hee sah-maj sak-tah.
(*I can't understand you.*)

MURPH   (*Repeating him in the same language*)   Toom-
haree bah-at nah-hee sah-maj sak-tah.

INDIAN   (*Recognizing the language finally. He speaks with
incredible speed*)   Toom-haree bah-sha nah-hee sah-
maj-tah. Moo-jhay mah-af kar-nah par ah-bhee moo-
jhay toom-ha-ray desh aye kuh-chah hee din toh Hu-
yay hain. Moo-jhay toom-ha-ree bah-sha see-kh-nay kah
ah-bhee sah-mai hee nah-hee milah. Mai ahp-nay lar-kay
say bih-chur gah-ya hoon. Oos-say toh toom-ha-ray desh
may rah-tay chai sah-al hoh gah-ye hain. Jah-b doh
mah-hee-nay pah-lay oos-kee mah kah inth-kahl moo-ah

toh oos-nay moo-jhay ya-han booh-lah bheh-jha or mai
ah gah-hay. Woh bah-ra hon-har lar-ka hai. Moo-jhay
mah-af kar-nah kee majh-nay ah-bhee toom-ha-ree bah-
sha na-hee see-knee par mai see-kh loon-gha.

> (*Yes, that's correct. I can't understand your lan-
> guage. I'm sorry, but I've only been in your country
> for a few days. I haven't had time to understand
> your language. Please forgive me. I'm separated
> from my son. He's been living in your country for
> six years. When his mother died two months ago, he
> sent for me. I came immediately. He's a good son to
> his father. I'm sorry I haven't learned your language
> yet, but I shall learn.*)

MURPH (*Does a take. Flatly*)   Thi.   rkie's a real pain in
the ass.

JOEY   Naw. I think he's pretty interes   . I never saw an
Indian before.

MURPH   Oh. It's fascinating. It's marvelc   This city's a
regular melting pot. Turkies. Kikes like   ,   (*Pause*) I
even had me a real French lady once. (ks at the
ground. Pauses*) I thought I saw a dime here   Ponders*)
I knew it.

> (*He picks up a dime and pockets it proudly*)

JOEY   A French lady, huh?

MURPH   Yep. A real French broad.

JOEY (*Holds a beat*)   You been at your mother again?

MURPH (*Hits him on the arm*)   Wise-ass. Just what nobody likes. A wise-ass.

144

JOEY Where'd you have this French lady, huh?

MURPH I found her in the park over there. (*Points*) Just sitting on a bench. She was great. (*Boasts*) A real *talent*.

JOEY Yeah, sure thing. (*Calls into the park*) Hello, talent. Hello, talent! (*Pauses*) I had a French girl, too. (*Turns to avoid* MURPH's *eyes, caught in a lie*) Where the hell's that bus?

MURPH (*Simply*) Sure you did. Like the time you had a mermaid?

JOEY You better believe I did. She wasn't really French. She just lived there a long time. I went to first grade with her. Geraldine. She was my first girl friend. (*Talks very quickly*) Her old man was in the Army or something, 'cause they moved to France. She came back when we were in high school.

MURPH Then what happened?

JOEY Nothin'. She just came back, that's all.

MURPH I thought you said you *had* her . . .

JOEY No, she was just my girl friend.

MURPH In high school?

JOEY No, ya stoop. In the first grade. I just told you.

MURPH You had her in the first grade?

JOEY Jesus, you're stupid. She was my girl friend. That's all.

MURPH (*Feigns excitement*) Hey . . . that's a *sweet little story*. (*Flatly*) What the hell's wrong with you?

JOEY What do ya' mean?

MURPH First you say you had a French girl, then you say you had a girl friend in first grade, who went to France. What the hell kind of story's that?

JOEY It's a true one, that's all. Yours is full of crap.

MURPH What's full of crap?

JOEY About the French lady in the park. You never had any French lady, unless you been at your own old lady again. Or maybe you've been at Pussyface?

MURPH Jesus, you're lookin' for it, aren't you?
(*They pretend to fistfight*)

JOEY I mean, if you gotta tell lies to your best buddy, you're in bad shape, that's all.

MURPH (*Gives* JOEY *a "high-sign"*) Best buddy? You?
(*The sign to* THE INDIAN. *He returns the obscene gesture, thinking it a berserk American sign of welcome*)

JOEY Is that how it is in Ceylon, sir?

MURPH Say-lon? What the hell is say-long?

JOEY See, ya jerk, Ceylon's part of India. That's where they grow tea.

INDIAN   Moo-jhay mah-af kar-nah. Mai toom-nakee bah-
sha na-hee sah-maj sak-ta.
   (*I'm sorry, but I can't understand your language.*)

MURPH   He's talking Indiana again. He don't understand.
Go on. Spin. I'll grab the Chief while you're spinning . . .
count the ten . . . hide the Chief, while you're after Pussyface. Go on. Spin.

JOEY   I ain't going to spin. I get sick.

MURPH   Ain't you going to play?

JOEY   I'll play. But I can't spin any better than you can. I
get sick. You know that. How about if you spin and I
hide the Chief? You can get Pussyface. She likes you better than me, anyhow.

MURPH   Pussyface ain't home. You know that. She's in
New Jersey.

JOEY   Then what the hell's the point of this game, anyway?

MURPH   It's just a game. We can pretend.

JOEY   You can play marbles for all I care. I just ain't going
to spin, that's all. And neither are you. So let's forget the
whole game.

MURPH (*Fiercely*)   Spin! Spin!

JOEY   You spin.

MURPH   Hey. I told you to spin.
   (MURPH *squares off against* JOEY *and slaps him*

149

menacingly. JOEY *looks* MURPH *straight in the eye
for a moment*)

JOEY   Okay. Big deal. So I'll spin. Then I get Pussyface,
right? You ready to get the Chief?

MURPH   Will you stop talking and start spinning?

JOEY   All right. All right. Here I go. (JOEY *spins himself
meekly, as* MURPH *goes toward* THE INDIAN *and the trash
can.* JOEY *giggles as he spins ever so slowly.* MURPH
glances at JOEY *as* JOEY *pretends.* MURPH *is confused*)
There. I spun. Is that okay?

MURPH   That's a spin?

JOEY   Well, it wasn't a fox trot.

MURPH   I told you to spin! Any slob knows that ain't no
spin! Now spin, God damn it! Spin!

JOEY   This is stupid. You want to play games. You want a
decent spin. You spin.
        (*He walks straight to* MURPH—*a challenge.* JOEY
slaps MURPH. *He winces*)

MURPH (*Squares off viciously. Raises his arms. Looks at*
JOEY *cruelly. Orders*)   Spin me.
        (JOEY *brings* MURPH's *arms behind* MURPH's *back
and holds* MURPH's *wrists firmly so that he is helpless.* JOEY *spins him. Slowly at first. Then faster.
Faster.* JOEY's *hostility is released; he laughs*)

JOEY   You wanted to spin. Spin. Spin.
        (JOEY *spins* MURPH *frantically.* THE INDIAN *watches*

> *in total horror, not knowing what to do; he cuddles*
> *next to the bus stop sign, his island of safety*)

MURPH (*Screaming*)   Enough, you little bastard.

JOEY (*Continues to spin him*)   Now *you* get Pussyface.
Go on. (*Spins* MURPH *all the faster as in a grotesque
dance gone berserk*) I'll hide the Chief. This is your
game! This is your game. *You* get Pussyface. I'll hide the
Chief. Go on, Murphy. You want some more spin? (JOEY
has stopped the spinning now, as MURPH *is obviously ill*)
You want to spin some more?

MURPH   Stop it, Joey. I'm sick.

JOEY (*Spins* MURPH *once more around*)   You want to spin
some more, or are you going to get Pussyface and come
find the Chief and me?

MURPH   You little bastard.

JOEY (*Spins* MURPH *once again, still holding* MURPH *helpless with his arms behind his back*)   I'll hide the Chief.
YOU get Pussyface and find us. Okay? Okay? Okay?

MURPH   Okay . . . you bastard . . . okay.

JOEY   Here's one more for good luck.
(JOEY *spins* MURPH *three more times, fiercely, then
shoves him offstage.* MURPH *can be heard retching,
about to vomit, during the final spins.* JOEY *then
grabs* THE INDIAN, *who pulls back in terror*)

INDIAN   Na-hee bha-yee toom ah-b k-yah kah-rogay?
(*No, please, what are you going to do?*)

JOEY   Easy, Chief. It's just a game. Murph spun out on us.
It's just a game. I've got to hide you now.
(MURPH's *final puking sounds can be heard well in
the distance*)

INDIAN   Na-hee na-hee bha-yee. Mai mah-afee mah-ng-ta.
Hoon.
(*No. No. Please. I beg you.*)

JOEY   Easy, Chief. Look. I promise you, this ain't for real.
This is only a game. A game. Get it? It's all a game! Now
I got to count to ten. (*Grabs* THE INDIAN *and forces him
down behind a city litter basket. He covers* THE INDIAN's
scream with his hand, as he slaps THE INDIAN—*a horrify-
ing sound*) One. Two. Three. Murphy? (*He laughs*)
Four. Five. Murph? Come get us. Six. Seven. Pussyface
is waiting. Eight. Nine. (*Pauses*) Murphy? Murph? Hey,
buddy. (*Stands up. Speaks*) Ten. (*Lights are narrowing
on* JOEY *and* THE INDIAN. THE INDIAN *tries to escape.* JOEY
subdues him easily. JOEY *turns slowly back to* THE IN-
DIAN, *who responds with open fear*) Get up. Up. (*No
response*) Get up, Turkie. (*Moves to* THE INDIAN, *who
recoils sharply.* JOEY *persists and pulls* THE INDIAN *to his
feet.* THE INDIAN *shudders, stands and faces his captor.*
THE INDIAN *shakes from fear and from a chill. There is a
moment's silence as* JOEY *watches. He removes his own
sweater and offers it to* THE INDIAN) Here. Here. Put it
on. It's okay. (THE INDIAN *is bewildered, but* JOEY *forces
the sweater into his hands*) Put it on. (THE INDIAN *stares
at the sweater.* JOEY *takes it from his hands and begins
to cover* THE INDIAN, *who is amazed*) I hope I didn't hurt
you too much. You okay? (*No response*) You ain't sick
too bad, huh? (*Pause*) Huh? (*Checks* THE INDIAN *for
cuts*) You look okay. You're okay, huh? (*No response*) I
didn't mean to rough you up like that, but . . . you know.

Huh? (THE INDIAN *raises his eyes to meet* JOEY'S. JOEY *looks down to avoid the stare*) I hope you ain't mad at me or nothin'. (*Pause*) Boy it's gettin' chilly. I mean, it's cold, right? Sure is quiet all of a sudden. Kind of spooky, huh? (*Calls*) Hey, Murphy! (*Laughs aloud*) Murph ain't a bad guy. He's my best buddy, see? I mean, he gets kinda crazy sometimes, but that's all. Everybody gets kind of crazy sometime, right? (*No response*) Jesus, you're a stupid Indian. Can't you speak any English? No? Why the hell did you come here, anyway? Especially if you can't talk any English. You ought to say something. Can't you even say "Thank you"?

> (THE INDIAN *recognizes those words, finally, and mimics them slowly and painfully*)

INDIAN (*In English, very British and clipped*)   Thank you.

JOEY   I'll be Goddamned! You're welcome. (*Slowly, indicating for* ⸋ INDIAN *to follow*) You're welcome.
(*He wa⸋*)

INDIAN (*In English*)   You are welcome.

JOEY   That's terrific. You⸋ welcome. (*Smiles, as though all is forgiven. In relief*) ⸋ w are you?

INDIAN   You are welcome.

JOEY   No. How are ya?
(JOEY *is excited.* THE INDIAN *might be a second friend*)

INDIAN (*In English—very "Joey"*)   How are ya?

JOEY (*Joyously*)   Jesus. You'll be talking like us in no time! You're okay, huh? You ain't bleeding or anything.

I didn't wanna hurt you none. But Murph gets all worked up. You know what I mean. He gets all excited. This ain't the first time, you know. No, sir!

INDIAN (*In English*)   No, sir.

JOEY   That's right. He's especially crazy around broads.

INDIAN (*In English*)   Broads.

JOEY (*Forgetting that* THE INDIAN *is only mimicking*) That's right. Broads. (*Pauses and remembers, deeply*) What am I yakking for? Tell me about India, huh? I'd like to go to India sometime. Maybe I will. You think I'd like India? India? (*No response.* THE INDIAN *recognizes the word, but doesn't understand the question*) That's where you're from, ain't it? Jesus, what a stupid Indian. India! (*Spells the word*) I-N-D-I-A. Nothin'. Schmuck. *India!*

INDIAN (*A stab in the dark*)   Hindi?

JOEY   Yeah! Tell me about India! (*Long pause as they stand staring at each other*) No? You're not talking, huh? Well, what do you want to do? Murph oughta be back soon. (*Discovers a coin in his pocket*) You wanna flip for quarters? Flip? No? Look, a Kennedy half! (*Goes through three magic tricks with the coin:* [1] *He palms the coin, offers the obvious choice of hand, then uncovers the coin in his other hand.* THE INDIAN *raises his hand to his turban in astonishment*) Like that, huh? ([2] *Coin is slapped on his breast*) This hand right? Is it this hand, this hand? No, it's *this* hand! Back to your dumb act? Here. Here's the one you liked! (*Does* [1]. *This time* THE INDIAN *points to the correct hand instantly*) You're probably some kind of hustler. Okay. Double or

nothing. (*Flips*) Heads, you live. Tails, you die. Okay?
(*Uncovers the coin*) I'll be a son of a bitch. You got
Indian luck. Here.
  (*He hands the coin to* THE INDIAN)

INDIAN (*Stares in question*)   Na-hff?
    (*No?*)

JOEY (*Considers cheating*)   Take it. You won. No, go
ahead. Keep it. I ain't no Indian giver. (*Pause. He laughs
at his own joke. No response*) You ain't got no sense of
humor, that's what. (*Stares upstage*) Murph's my best
buddy, you know? Me and him were buddies when we
were kids. Me and Murph, all the time. And Maggie. His
kid sister. (*Pause*) I had Maggie once. Sort of. Well, kind
of. Yeah, I had her. That's right. Murph don't know.
Makes no difference now. She's dead, Maggie. (*Sings*)
"The worms crawl in, the worms crawl out." (*Speaks*)
What the hell difference does it make? *Right?*

INDIAN (*In English*)   No, sir.

JOEY (*Without noticing*)   Th 's why Murph is crazy.
That's why he gets crazy, I m   n. She died seventeen,
that's all. Seventeen. Just like ɪ ut. Appendix. No one
around. There was no one around. His old lady? Forget
it! The old man took off years ago.   'll there was really
was just Murph and Maggie. That's   v he could take
it. At home. You think my old lady's   '? She's nothing. His old lady's a pro. You know? She d   't even make
a living at it, either. That's the bitch of it. Not even a
living. She's a dog. I mean, *I* wouldn't even pay her a
nickel. Not a nickel. Not that I'd screw around with
Murphy's old lady. Oh! Not that she doesn't try. She
tries. Plenty. (*His fantasy begins*) That's why I don't

come around to his house much. She tries it all the time. She wouldn't charge me anything, probably. But it ain't right screwing your best buddy's old lady, right? I'd feel terrible if I did. She ain't that bad, but it just ain't right. I'd bet she'd even take Murph on. She probably tries it with him, too. That's the bitch of it. She can't even make a living. His own Goddamned mother. The other one— Pussyface. You think Pussyface is a help? That's the biggest joke yet. (THE INDIAN *is by now thoroughly confused on all counts. He recognizes the name "Pussyface," and reacts slightly. Seeing* JOEY'S *anxiety, he cuddles him. For a brief moment they embrace—an insane father-and-son tableau. Note: Be careful here*) Pussyface. There's a brain. You see what she gave us for Christmas? (*Fishes his knife out of his pocket*) Knives. Brilliant, huh? Murph's up on a rap for slicing a kid, and she gives us knives for Christmas. To whittle with. She's crazier th.. Murphy. Hah. (*Flashes his open knife at* THE INDIAN, *whc misinterprets the move as spelling disaster.* THE INDIAN *waits, carefully scrutinizing* JOEY, *until* JOEY *begins to look away.* JOEY *now wanders to the spot where he pushed* MURPH *offstage*) Hey, Murph! (THE INDIAN *moves slowly to the other side of the stage.* JOEY *sees his move at once and races after him, thinking* THE INDIAN *was running away*) Hey. Where are you going? (THE INDIAN *knows he'll be hit. He tries to explain with mute gestures and attitude. It's futile. He knows at once and hits* JOEY *as best he can and races across the stage.* JOEY *recovers from the blow and starts after him, as* THE INDIAN *murmurs one continuous frightening scream.* JOEY *dives after* THE INDIAN *and tackles him on the other side of the stage.* THE INDIAN *fights more strongly than ever, but* JOEY'S *trance carries him ferociously into this fight. He batters* THE INDIAN *with punches to the body.* THE INDIAN *squeals as* JOEY *sobs*) You were gonna run

off. Right? Son of a bitch. You were gonna tell Murphy.
(THE INDIAN *makes one last effort to escape and runs
the length of the stage, screaming a bloodcurdling,
anguished scream.* MURPH *enters, stops, stares incredulously as* THE INDIAN *runs into his open arms.*
JOEY *races to* THE INDIAN *and strikes a karate chop
to the back of his neck.* JOEY *is audibly sobbing.* THE
INDIAN *drops to the stage as a bull in the ring, feeling
the final thrust of the sword . . .* JOEY *stands frozen
above him.* MURPH *stares, first at* JOEY *and then at*
THE INDIAN)

MURPH   Pussyface isn't home yet. She's still in New Jersey.
Ring-a-leave-eo.

JOEY (*Sobbing, senses his error*)   Indians are dumb.

MURPH (*Stares again at* JOEY. *Then to* THE INDIAN. *Spots*
JOEY's *sweater on* THE INDIAN. *Fondles it, then stares at*
JOEY *viciously*)   Pussyface isn't home. I rang her bell.
She don't answer. I guess she's still on vacation. She
ruined our game.

JOEY (*Sobbing*)   Oh, jumping Jesus Christ. Jesu   Jesus.
Jesus. Indians are dumb.

MURPH   Pussyface ruins everything. She don't really ⟨ ⟩
about our games. She ruins our games. Just like India⟨ ⟩
They don't know how to play our games either.

JOEY   Indians are dumb. Dumb.
(*He sobs.* MURPH *slaps* JOEY *across the face. He
straightens up and comes back to reality*)

MURPH   What the hell's going on?

157

JOEY   He tried to run. I hit him.

MURPH   Yeah. I saw that. You hit him, all right. (*Stares at* THE INDIAN) Is he alive?
(THE INDIAN *groans, pulls himself to his knees*)

JOEY   He was fighting. I hit him.

MURPH   Okay, you hit him.
(THE INDIAN *groans again. Then he speaks in a plea*)

INDIAN   (*Praying*)   Moo-jhay or nah sah-tao. Maih-nay toom-hara k-yah bigarah hai. Moo-jhay or nah sah-tao. Moo-jhay in-seh.
(*Please. Don't hurt me any more. What have I done? Please don't hurt me. Don't let them hurt me*)

MURPH   He's begging for something. Maybe he's begging for his life. Maybe he is. Sure, maybe he is.

JOEY   (*Embarrassed, starts to help* THE INDIAN *to his feet*) C'mon there, Chief. Get up and face the world. C'mon, Chief. Everything's going to be all right.

MURPH   What's got into you, anyway?

JOEY   C'mon, Chief. Up at the world. Everything's okay.
(THE INDIAN *ad libs words of pleading and pain*)

MURPH   Leave him be. (*But* JOEY *continues to help* THE INDIAN) Leave him be. What's with you? Hey, Joey! I said leave him be!
(MURPH *pushes* JOEY *and* THE INDIAN *pulls back with fear*)

JOEY   Okay, Murph. Enough's enough.

MURPH   Just tell me what the hell's wrong with you?

JOEY   He tried to run away, that's all. Change the subject. Change the subject. It ain't important. I hit him, that's all.

MURPH   Okay, so you hit him.

JOEY   Okay! Where were you? Sick. Were you a little bit sick? I mean, you couldn't have been visiting, 'cause there ain't no one to visit, right?

MURPH   What *do* you mean?

JOEY   Where the hell were you? (*Looks at* MURPH *and giggles*) You're a little green there, Irish.

MURPH   You're pretty funny. What the hell's so funny?

JOEY   Nothing's funny. The Chief and I were just having a little pow-wow and we got to wondering where you ran off to. Just natural for us to wonder, ain't it? (*To* THE INDIAN) Right, Chief.

MURPH   Hey, look at that. Turkie's got a woolly sweater just like yours. Ain't that a terrific coincidence. You two been playing strip poker?

JOEY   Oh, sure. Strip poker. The Chief won my sweater and I won three of his feathers and a broken arrow. (*To* THE INDIAN, *he feigns a deep authoritative voice*) You wonder who I am, don't you? Perhaps this silver bullet will help to identify me? (*Extends his hand.* THE INDIAN *peers into* JOEY's *empty palm quizzically. As he does,* MURPH *quickly taps the underside of* JOEY's *hand, forc-*

ing the hand to rise and slap THE INDIAN'*s chin sharply.*
THE INDIAN *pulls back at the slap.* JOEY *turns on* MURPH,
quickly) What the hell did you do that for, ya' jerk. The
Chief didn't do nothing.

MURPH   Jesus, you and your Chief are pretty buddy-
buddy, ain't you? (*Mimics* JOEY) "The Chief didn't do
nothing." Jesus. You give him your sweater. Maybe you'd
like to have him up for a beer . . .

JOEY   Drop it, Murph. You're giving me a pain in the ass.

MURPH   (*Retorts fiercely*)   You little pisser. Who the hell
do you think you're talking to?
      (*The telephone rings in the booth. They are all star-
      tled, especially* THE INDIAN, *who senses hope*)

JOEY   (*After a long wait, speaking the obvious flatly*)   It's
the phone.

MURPH   (*To* THE INDIAN)   The kid's a whiz. He guessed
that right away.
      (*The phone rings a second time*)

JOEY   Should we answer it?

MURPH   What for? W.. 'd be calling here? It's a wrong
number.
      (*The phone rings menacingly a third time. Sud-
      denly* THE INDIAN *darts into the phone booth and
      grabs the receiver.* JOEY *and* MURPH *are too startled
      to stop him until he has blurted out his hopeless
      plea, in his own language*)

INDIAN   Prem k-yah woh may-rah ar-kah hai. Prem (pray-
em) bay-tah moo-jhay bachah-low. Mai fah ns ga-yah

hoon yeh doh goon-day moo-jhay mar ra-hay hain. Mai
ba-hoot ghah-bara gaya hoon. Pray-em.

(*Prem? Is this my son? Prem? Please help me. I'm
frightened. Please help me. Two boys are hurting
me . . . I'm frightened. Please. Prem?*)

(THE INDIAN *stops talking sharply and listens. He
crumbles as the voice drones the wrong reply. He
drops the receiver and stares with horror at the
boys.* MURPH *realizes* THE INDIAN's *horror and begins
to laugh hysterically.* JOEY *stares silently.* THE IN-
DIAN *begins to mumble and weep. He walks from
the phone booth. The voice is heard as a drone from
the receiver. The action freezes*)

MURPH (*Laughing*) What's the matter, Turkie? Don't
you have a dime? Give Turkie a dime, Joe. Give him a
dime.

JOEY Jesus Christ. I'd hate to be an Indian.

MURPH Hey, the paper! C'mon, Joey, get the paper from
him. We'll call the Bronx.

JOEY Cut it out, Murph. Enough's enough.

MURPH Get the frigging piece of paper. What's the matter with you, anyway?

JOEY I just don't think it's such a terrific idea, that's all.

MURPH You're chicken. That's what you are.

JOEY Suppose his son has called the police. What do you
think? You think he hasn't called the police? He knows

the old man don't speak any English. He called the police. Right? And they'll trace our call.

MURPH You're nuts. They can't trace any phone calls. Anyway, we'll be gone from here. You're nuts.

JOEY I don't want to do it.

MURPH For Christ's sake. They can't trace nothing to nobody. Who's going to trace? Get the paper.

JOEY Get it yourself. Go on. Get it yourself. I ain't going to get it.

MURPH C'mon, Joey. It's not real. This is just a game. It ain't going to hurt anybody. You know that. It's just a game.

JOEY Why don't we call somebody else? We'll call somebody else and have the Indian talk. That makes sense. Imagine if an Indian called you up and talked to you in Indian. I bet the Chief would go for that all right. Jesus, Murphy.

MURPH Get the paper and picture.

INDIAN Ah-b toom k-yah kah-rogay. Moo-jhay mah-af kar-doh bha-yee maih-nay soh-cha tah key woh may-rah bay-tah pray-em hai. Moo-jhay telephone kar raha. Mai-nay soh-chah thah sha-yahd woh. Pray-em hoh.
    (*What are you going to do now? I'm sorry. I thought that was my son, Prem. I thought that it might be Prem calling me on the telephone. Prem. That's who I thought it was. Prem.*)

162

MURPH   Prem. That's the name.
    (*Plays the rhyme*)

INDIAN   Pray-aim.
    (*Prem?*)

MURPH   Yes, Prem. I want to call Prem. Give me the paper
with his name.

INDIAN   Toom pray-aim kay ba-ray may k-yah kah ra-hay.
Ho toom-nay pray-aim koh kyah key-yah. Toom oos-
kay bah-ray may k-yah jan-tay ho k-yah toom jan-tay
ho woh kah-han hai.
    (*What are you saying about Prem? Prem is my son.
What have you done to Prem? What do you know
about him? Do you know where he is?*)

MURPH   Shut up already and give me the paper.

JOEY   Jesus, Murph.

MURPH (*Turning* THE INDIAN *around so that they face each
other*)   This is ridiculous. (*Searches* THE INDIAN, *who
resists a bit at first, and then not at all. Finally,* MURPH
finds the slip of paper) I got it. I got it. Terrific. "Prem
Gupta." In the Bronx. In the frigging Bronx. This is terrific. (*Pushes* THE INDIAN *to* JOEY) Here. Hold him.

INDIAN   Toom k-yah kar ra-hay ho k-yah toom pray-aim
k-oh boo-lah ra-hay ho.
    (*What are you doing? Are you going to call my
son?*)

MURPH   Shut him up. (*Fishes for a dime*) Give me a dime,
God damn it. This is terrific.

JOEY (*Finds the coins in his pocket*)   Here's two nickels. (*Hands them over*) I think this is a rotten idea, that's what I think. (*Pauses*) And don't forget to pay me back those two nickels either.

MURPH   Just shut up. (*Dials the information operator*) Hello. Yeah, I want some information . . . I want a number up in the Bronx . . . Gupta . . . G-U-P-T-A . . . an Indian kid . . . His first name's Prem . . . P-R-E-M . . . No . . . I can't read the street right . . . Wait a minute. (*Reads the paper to himself*) For Christ's sake. How many Indians are up in the Bronx? There must be only one Indian named Gupta.

JOEY   What's she saying?

MURPH   There are two Indians named Gupta. (*To the operator*) Is the two of them named Prem? (*Pauses*) Well, that's what I told you . . . Jesus . . . wait a minute . . . okay . . . okay. Say that again . . . Okay . . . Okay . . . Right. Okay . . . thanks. (*Hurries quickly to return the coins to the slot.* GUPTA *mumbles. To* JOEY) Don't talk to me. (*Dials*) Six . . . seven-four. Oh. One. Seven, seven. (*Pauses*) It's ringing. It's ringing. (*Pauses*) Hello. (*Covers the phone with his hand*) I got him! Hello? Is this Prem Gupta? Oh swell. How are you? (*To* JOEY) I got the kid!

>   (THE INDIAN *breaks from* JOEY's *arm and runs to the telephone . . .* MURPH *sticks out his leg and holds* THE INDIAN *off.* THE INDIAN *fights, but seems weaker than ever*)

INDIAN (*Screams*)   Cree-payah moo-jhay ad-nay lar-kay say bah-at kar-nay doh.

>   (*Please let me talk to my son.*)

>   (MURPH *slams* THE INDIAN *aside violently.* JOEY

stands frozen, watching. THE INDIAN *wails and finally talks calmly, as in a trance)* Cree-payah moo-jhay ahd-nay lar-kay say bah-at kar-nay doh. Mai toom-haray hah-th jor-tah hoom mai toom-hay joh mango-gay doon-gar bus moo-jhay oos-say bah-at kar-nay doh.

(*Please let me talk to my son. Oh, Prem. Please, I beg of you. Please. I'll give you anything at all. Just tell me what you want of me. Just let me talk with my son. Won't you, please?*)

(MURPH *glares at* THE INDIAN, *who no longer tries to interfere, as it becomes obvious that he must listen to even the language he cannot understand*)

MURPH   Just listen to me, will you, Gupta? I don't know where the hell your old man is, that's why I'm calling. We found an old elephant down here in Miami and we thought it must be yours. You can't tell for sure whose elephant is whose. You know what I mean? (MURPH *is laughing now*) What was that? Say that again. I can't hear you too well. All the distance between us, you know what I mean? It's a long way down here, you follow me? No. I ain't got no Indian. I just got an elephant. And he's eating all my peanuts. Gupta, you're talking too fast. Slow down.

INDIAN   Pray-aim bhai-yah moo-jhay ah-kay lay ja-oh moo-jhay ap-nay lar-kay say bah-at kar-nay doh moo-jhay oos-say bah-at k-yohn nah-hee kar-nay day-tay.

(*Prem! Prem! Please come and get me. Please let me talk to my son, mister. Why don't you let me talk to my son?*)

(JOEY *leaps on* THE INDIAN; *tackles him, lays on top of him in front of the telephone booth*)

165

MURPH   That was the waiter. I'm in an Indian restaurant. (*Pauses*) Whoa. Slow down, man. That was nobody. That was just a myth. Your imagination. (*Pauses. Screams into the receiver*) Shut up, damn you! And listen. Okay? Okay. Are you listening? (MURPH *tastes the moment. He silently clicks the receiver back to the hook. To* JOEY) He was very upset. (*To* THE INDIAN) He was very upset. (*Pauses*) Well, what the hell's the matter with you? I only told him we found an elephant, that's all. I thought maybe he lost his elephant.

(THE INDIAN *whimpers*)

INDIAN   Toom-nay ai-saw k-yohn ki-yah toom-nay may-ray lar-kay koh k-yah ka-hah hai.

(*Why have you done this? What have you said to my son?*)

MURPH   You don't have to thank me, Turkie. I only told him your elephant was okay. He was probably worried sick about your elephant. (MURPH *laughs*) This is terrific, Joey. Terrific. You should have heard the guy jabber. He was so excited he started talking in Indian just like the Chief. He said that Turkie here and him got separated today. Turkie's only been in the city one day. You're pretty stupid, Turkie. One day in the city . . . and look at the mess you've made. You're pretty stupid. He's stupid, right?

JOEY   Yeah. He's stupid.

MURPH   Hold him. We'll try again. Sure.

(THE INDIAN *jumps on* MURPH. *He tries to strangle* MURPH)

MURPH (*Screaming*)   Get him off of me! (JOEY *pulls* THE INDIAN *down to the ground as* MURPH *pounds the booth*

166

four times, screaming hideous sounds of aggression. With this tension released he begins to call, fierce but controlled, too controlled. MURPH *takes the dime from his pocket, shows it to* JOEY, *and recalls the number. Talking into receiver. He dials number again and waits for reply.*) Hello? Is this Gupta again? Oh, hello there . . . I'm calling back to complain about your elephant . . . hey, slow down, will you? Let me do the talking. Okay? Your elephant is a terrific pain in the balls to me, get it? Huh? Do you follow me so far? (*Pauses*) I don't know what you're saying, man . . . how about if I do the talking, all right? . . . Your elephant scares hell out of me and my pal here. We don't like to see elephants on the street. Spiders and snakes are okay, but elephants scare us. Elephants . . . yeah, that's right. Don't you get it, pal? . . . Look, we always see spiders and snakes. But we never expect to see an elephant . . . What do you mean "I'm crazy"? I don't know nothing about your old man . . . I'm talking about your elephant. Your elephant offends the hell out of me. So why don't you be a nice Indian kid and come pick him up . . . that's right . . . wait a minute . . . I'll have to check the street sign. (*Covers the receiver*) This is terrific. (*Talks again into the telephone*) Jesus, I'm sorry about that. There don't seem to be no street sign . . . that's a bitch. I guess you lose your elephant . . . well, what do you expect me to do, bring your elephant all the way up to the Bronx? Come off it, pal. You wouldn't ever bring my elephant home. I ain't no kid, you know! I've lost a couple of elephants in my day. (*Listens*) Jesus, you're boring me now . . . I don't know what the hell you're talking about. Maybe you want to talk to your elephant . . . huh? (*Turns to* THE INDIAN) Here, come talk to your "papoose."

(*He offers the telephone.* THE INDIAN *stares in dis-*

belief, then grabs the telephone from MURPH's *hands and begins to chatter wildly)*

INDIAN Pray-aim, bhai-yah Pray-aim moo-jhay ah-kay lay jah-oh k-yah? Moo-jhay nah-hee pa-tah mai kah-han hoo-n moo-jhay ah-hp-nay gha-ar lay chah-low ya-hahn do-ah bad-mash lar-kay. Jo bah-hoot kha-tar-nahk hai-don-say mai nah-hee bah-cha sak-tah ah-pa-nay koh toom aik-dam moo-jhay ah-kay.

> *(Prem? Oh, Prem. Please come and take me away . . . what? I don't know where I am . . . Please come and take me to your house . . . please? There are two bad people. Two young men. They are dangerous. I cannot protect myself from them. Please . . . You must come and get me.)*

> *(*MURPH *takes his knife from his pocket, cuts the line.* THE INDIAN *almost falls flat on his face as the line from the receiver to the phone box is cut, since he has been leaning away from* MURPH *and* JOEY *during his plea)*

MURPH You've had enough, Chief.
> *(*MURPH *laughs aloud)*

INDIAN *(Not at once realizing the line must be connected, continues to talk into the telephone in Hindi)* Pray-aim, Pray-aim, ya-hahn aa-oh sah-rak kah nah-am hai—yeh toom-nay k-yah key-yah.

> *(Prem. Prem. Please come here. The street sign reads . . .)*

> *(He now realizes he has been cut off and stares dumbly at the severed cord as* MURPH *waves the severed cord in his face)*
Toom-nay yeh k-yoh key-yah?
> *(What have you done?)*

MURPH   There it is, Turkie. Who you talkin' to?

INDIAN   (*To* JOEY, *screaming a father's fury and disgust*)
Toom-nay yeh k-yohn key-yah cri-payah may-ree mah-
dah-d kah-roho.
(*Why have you done this? Please. Please help me.*)

(JOEY *has been standing throughout the entire
scene, frozen in terror and disgust. He walks slowly
toward* MURPH, *who kicks* THE INDIAN. JOEY *bolts
from the stage, muttering one continuous droning
sob*)

MURPH   (*Screaming*)   Go ahead, Joey. Love him. Love
him like a mother. Hey? Joey? What the hell's the matter? C'mon, buddy? (*Turns to* THE INDIAN, *takes his knife
and cuts* THE INDIAN'S *hand, so blood is on the knife*)
Sorry, Chief. This is for my buddy, Joey. And for Pussyface. (*Calls offstage*) Joey! Buddy! What the hell's the
matter? (*Races from the stage after* JOEY) Joey! Wait
up. Joey! I killed the Indian!
(*He exits.* THE INDIAN *stares dumbly at his hand,
dripping blood. He then looks to the receiver and
talks into it*)

INDIAN   Pray-aim, Pray-aim, mai ah-pa-nay lar-kay key
ah-wah-az k-yon nah-hee soon sak-tah Pray-aim! Toom-
nay may-ray sah-ahth aih-saw k-yohn key-yaw bay-tah
Pray-aim, k-yah toom ho?
(*Prem. Prem.*)

(*He walks center stage, well away from the telephone booth*)

(*Why can I not hear my son, Prem? Why have you
done this to me?*)

(*Suddenly the telephone rings again. Once. Twice.* THE INDIAN *is startled. He talks into the receiver, while he holds the dead line in his bleeding hand*) (*Prem? Is that you? Prem?*)

(*The telephone rings a third time*) Pray-aim, Pray-aim, bay-tah k-yah toom ho—
(*Prem. Prem? Is that you?*)

(*A fourth ring.* THE INDIAN *knows the telephone is dead*) Pray-aim Pray-aim—moo-jhay bah-chald Pray-aim.
(*Prem. Prem. Help me. Prem.*)

(*As the telephone rings a fifth time, in the silence of the night, the sounds of two boys' singing is heard*)

FIRST BOY
I walk the lonely streets at night,
A'lookin' for your door . . .

SECOND BOY
I look and look and look and look . . .

FIRST BOY *and* SECOND BOY
But, baby, you don't care.
But, baby, no one cares.
But, baby, no one cares.
(*Their song continues to build as they repeat the lyrics, so the effect is one of many, many voices. The telephone continues its unanswered ring.* THE INDIAN *screams a final anguished scream of fury to the boys offstage.*

The telephone rings a final ring as THE INDIAN *screams*)

INDIAN (*Desperately, holding the telephone to the audience as an offer. He speaks in English into the telephone. The only words he remembers are those from his lesson*)

How are you? You're welcome. You're welcome. Thank you. (*To the front*) Thank you!

Blackout

rats /

"Caesar! Christ! Jack!
Martin! Bobby! What's
happening to us?"

Anon.

Rats: Scott Glenn as BOBBY, Tom Scott as BABY,
and Tom Rosqui as JEBBIE.

RATS *was first presented by Lyn Austin, Oliver Smith and Hale Mathews on April 18, 1968, at The Loft Workshop, New York City, for preview performances with the following cast:*

(In order of appearance)	JEBBIE	Tom Rosqui
	BOBBY	Scott Glenn
	BABY	Tom Scott

Directed by   Edward Parone

Subsequently RATS *was presented with the same cast and director on May 8, 1968, as the final play on a bill of twelve plays entitled* Collision Course, *at Café Au Go Go, New York City.*

Setting: The interior of a baby's crib. Harlem.
Time: Unfortunately, the present.

The stage is dark and without scenery. A single saxophone chord is heard; the lights come up on JEBBIE, *a fat Harlem rat, who sits, legs crossed, counting money.*

JEBBIE   One dollar. One peseta. One mark. One kroner. One shilling. (*Suddenly he senses the presence of another rat. He leaps up and runs about the stage frantically. Yelling*) Where are you? Who's there? C'mon out, God damn it. I know you're here. Come out and show yourself. Show yourself. (*A second rat enters*—BOBBY. *He's younger and thinner than* JEBBIE. *They circle each other cautiously.* JEBBIE *is obviously stronger;* BOBBY, *frightened*) There you are. I knew it!

BOBBY   Please. Please. Please don't. (*They continue to circle each other.* JEBBIE *jabs at* BOBBY, *who pulls back each time*) Please help me.

JEBBIE   What do you want?

BOBBY   I want in.

JEBBIE   Out! Out!

BOBBY   In. I want in. Please.

JEBBIE   Out, like the rest of them! Out!

BOBBY   Listen. I'm sorry. I mean, I don't want to interrupt you or trouble you. Bother you. I can see you're busy. (*Pauses*) You've got to help me.

179

JEBBIE   Out! Out! Out of my place, kid! Find your own, kid!

BOBBY   Charlie "ratted" on his brother!

JEBBIE   Don't play on my sympathy. Out!

BOBBY   He's a dirty rat!

JEBBIE   Don't play on my sympathy.

BOBBY   I smell a rat!

JEBBIE   Don't play that game with me, kid. I was a kid, kid. I heard all them expressions. They don't affect me now. Find your own way. Find your own place. Out!

BOBBY   Rats spelled backward is *star!*

JEBBIE   Out!

BOBBY   Please. You gotta help me. (*They continue to circle each other, but much more slowly now*) It took me weeks to get up here. Weeks to find you. So I could talk with you. Be with you. Please. You've got to help me! Please. You got to!

JEBBIE   I don't *gotta* do anything, pal.

BOBBY   I know that. I know how busy you are. Look, I want in. I want in so much it's killing me. Please don't hate me for not knocking. For just running in on you, but I need help. I really need help.

JEBBIE   (*Assuming the posture of a businessman*)   Look, when I was a kid, struggling like a son of a bitch, I needed help, right?

BOBBY   I would have helped you.

JEBBIE   Yeah. Sure.

BOBBY   Listen, please. I would have. I help everybody I can. (*Digs into his pocket. Pulls out a huge chunk of cheese and offers it to* JEBBIE) Here.

JEBBIE   You've got to be kidding.

BOBBY (*Finds two other pieces*)   I heard there was a lack of cheeses.

JEBBIE   Cheeses! Maybe you need help, kid, but you ain't getting me into a helpful mood. What do you want?

BOBBY (*Confused that his gift has been rejected*)   Cheeses from the finest estate in Greenwich.

JEBBIE   Cheeses in the Village?

BOBBY   The Village?

JEBBIE   That's what you said. "Cheeses from the finest whatever in Greenwich."

BOBBY (*Guilty*)   Greenwich, Connecticut.

JEBBIE (*Enraged*)   That kind of help! Another one. Look. I'll hold my temper down. But I gotta tell you, kid, I'm hip to your problem because I get calls from two hundred little madras-commuting-blond-Nazi-gold bless-America mice like you every week. I'm hip to your problem, but I don't want to help and I ain't gonna help. Where the Christ do you think I was born? The Bronx? Avenue A? I pulled my ass up from Jersey. That's right,

Jersey. Not Newark, either, so don't get any smart ideas. I started right at the bottom, baby.

BOBBY   South Orange?

JEBBIE   Worse.

BOBBY   Montclair?

JEBBIE   C'mon, that's nothing.

BOBBY   My God, where?

JEBBIE   Now tell me why I should tell you? Huh? I've got friends I've never told. Why should I tell you?

BOBBY   My mother left me those cheeses.

JEBBIE   Huh?

BOBBY   My mother left me those cheeses. In her will.

JEBBIE   Your mother?

BOBBY   She got it. I saw the seeds. I told her not to eat them. I was only a kid, but I knew. "Don't eat them, Mama. Please." (*Now weeping*) "Don't eat the seeds, Mama. I think it's the stuff." It was bad for us. We were all skinny. Hungry. I begged her to eat the cheeses. Begged her. But she was my mother. Things were bad. She said . . . she said . . . (*He breaks down, crying*)

JEBBIE (*Walks over and stares at* BOBBY)   Okay. Sit down.

BOBBY   I wasn't going to cry. I haven't cried for fifteen months.

JEBBIE   Don't believe that crap about not crying. Men can cry. Go on. Cry your ass off. No one's gonna know. There's nobody here. No one's gonna know.

BOBBY   I'm all right now. I'm all right. I can't understand it. I haven't cried for fifteen months. Not since my father told me how things were. What I was. You know what I mean?

JEBBIE   Look, kid. I said it was okay to cry. Go on. Cry like a man. That's what *they* don't know. That's a big thing we've got going on them. It's okay. Whine. Cry. Go on.

BOBBY   (*Weeping, then crying, he reaches out for* JEBBIE *to hold him*)   I'm lonely, I'm scared.

JEBBIE   Don't touch me. Hey. Don't touch me! (*Pulls back quickly, in a strange frightened move as* BOBBY *threatens to embrace him*) Go on. Cry. Cry like a man. Get all them tears out good. Just sit over there and cry, kid. It'll do you good. Damn good.

BOBBY   I'm better now. Jesus, just being here with you makes me better. The loneliness started to go away as I started to get closer to this place. I'm okay now.

JEBBIE   Star spelled backwards, huh? When'd you figure that one out?

BOBBY   Hell. When I was thirteen or so. I told my folks, and they laughed and laughed and laughed.

JEBBIE   Superstar is Repusrats! (*Considers it*) That don't make any sense.

BOBBY   I ain't normally like this. I got myself kind of worked up. I walked all the way here by myself. All the way from Greenwich. It's a long way. I got myself tired. I got worked up. I saw others like us in the sewers on the way. They got me worked up. Scared that it was all a mistake. I got scared. I got this awful feeling all over me, like I just wanted to lay down and cry, and maybe die. You know?

JEBBIE   Sure, kid. I know. (*Pauses*) Let's eat some of those cheeses, huh?

BOBBY   (*Thrilled. Simply*)   Thank you.

JEBBIE   Don't start any of your sweet stuff on me. I'm hungry, that's all.

BOBBY   (*Gives* JEBBIE *his cheese*)   See? Three kinds.

JEBBIE   I ain't gonna eat alone.

BOBBY   But they're a gift.

JEBBIE   You're a dumb little bastard, you know that? You got to me. Got me going with you. Don't screw it all around trying to brown-nose me now. You're hungry? Eat. You ain't hungry? Take your cheeses and fuck off.

BOBBY   I'm sorry. I'm sorry if you think I'm brown-nosing or sucking around or anything like that. Look, I want to be honest with you. I wouldn't just give you my cheeses if I didn't want something from you, right? That's honest, isn't it?

JEBBIE   (*Delighted*)   You're all right, kid. You're definitely

184

all right. That's straight talk. That's good. (*Tries the cheese*) That's good cheese, too.

BOBBY   You see, my mother knew it would do me some good someday. Get me out of the mess. You know what I mean? So she ate the seeds.

JEBBIE   Suicide, huh?

BOBBY   No. That's just it. Suicide's beautiful. For us, I mean. (*Pauses*) I really am paranoid.

JEBBIE   What's that?

BOBBY   Paranoid. That's one of those words you learn . . .

JEBBIE   One of *them* words you learn!

BOBBY   Yeah. One of *them* words you learn when you're on the skids. Greenwich. Anywhere in Fairfield County. It just means that you imagine bad things that maybe aren't entirely true.

JEBBIE   There's your first lesson. You think I don't know what "paranoid" means? Huh? I know lots of big words.

BOBBY   I don't get it.

JEBBIE   Penis envy.

BOBBY   My God!

JEBBIE   That's nothing. Listen. (*Lays the words out slowly*) Nursery school. Caviar. *Schvatza.*

BOBBY   You weren't kidding, were you?

185

JEBBIE (*Checks to see if anyone could possibly overhear him, and then speaks rapidly, as a typewriter*) Bulls. Bears. Sell short. Capital gains. Account executive. Copy supervisor. Underwriter. (*The clincher*) Air Travel Card.

BOBBY That recently, huh?

JEBBIE What do you mean?

BOBBY That recently. Just what I said. You must have been there within the last eighteen months.

JEBBIE (*Shocked*) How'd you know?

BOBBY Air Travel Cards. They're fairly new. Not two decades, even.

JEBBIE (*Amazed and delighted*) Hey. You're a pretty smart kid.

BOBBY I'm no kid.

JEBBIE You look like a kid.

BOBBY I'm twenty-five.

JEBBIE You're kidding.

BOBBY I know. I've always looked nine.

JEBBIE Hell, I'm twenty-nine. Twenty-five's a kid in my book.

BOBBY My grandfather went all the way to thirty-nine.

JEBBIE (*Incredulously*)   Thirty-nine months old?

BOBBY   Yes. (*Corrects himself*) Yep. Thirty-nine months and three days, to the minute. And he bought it with barium chloride too.

JEBBIE   No shit.

BOBBY (*Delighted by* JEBBIE's *language*)   No shit! 'Course, he was down in Georgia. The heat helps.

JEBBIE   Yeah, but thirty-nine.

BOBBY   Terrific, huh?

JEBBIE   He must have come over on the *Mayflower*.

BOBBY   Way back they did.

JEBBIE   Maybe you ought to stay in Greenwich.

BOBBY (*Hurt by that insult.* JEBBIE *withdraws*)   C'mon kid. You've got to have a sense of humor. Hell. What's your name?

BOBBY   Bobby.

JEBBIE   That's okay. I'm Jebbie.

BOBBY   You think I don't know that?

JEBBIE (*Extremely pleased*)   That's what you call your modesty. I guess everybody knows me, huh?

BOBBY   You're a legend in Fairfield County.

187

JEBBIE   I'll give you your first lesson, Bobby. You don't get famous by waiting for somebody to do anything for you. You got to fight it out yourself, kid. You gotta fight dirty and tough. None of us got to be anything by not playing it dirty, Bobby. You think your grandfather went to thirty-nine by being a nice-guy? Shit, no! He must have known the game. When to bite and kill. When to play it cool.

BOBBY   He was tough, all right.

JEBBIE   See this scar? You're privileged, Bobby. That scar's from a kid just like you. Wanted to take over, Bobby. Wanted Jebbie's place. But I got him, Bobby.

BOBBY   Oh, wow! Teeth?

JEBBIE   Forget it. Don't think about it. We got it from all sides, kid. If the others don't get you, your own will.

BOBBY   I felt that. I felt it in the sewers coming up here. They scared me, Jebbie. Something awful.

JEBBIE   You fight and you fight and you fight. But one day you wake up, and if you've fought 'em all hard enough, you've made it. You have a place that's all your own. You have money. Food. All the stuff you think you'll never get, you get. If you fight hard enough.

BOBBY   I want to learn; honest. I want to learn.

JEBBIE   You gotta learn things nobody ever told you about. Believe me. Things nobody ever told you about.

BOBBY   But I want to. I want to.

JEBBIE   Barium, huh?

BOBBY   Oh, yeah. Thirty-nine.

JEBBIE   That's how my old lady got it.

BOBBY   Your mother?

JEBBIE   Naw. My old lady. The missus. Barium chloride. Then they got the kids.

BOBBY   I'm sorry. Big family?

JEBBIE   Not huge. Not bad. Just nice. We had sixty kids. That was a beautiful year. Then she got it first. I couldn't handle the kids on my own. Funny the way things happen. I went off for about five minutes. We were in Jersey. I told you that.

BOBBY   You didn't tell me what town.

JEBBIE   Upper Montclair. You were pretty close.

BOBBY   Upper Montclair!!! Jesus Christ. Upper Montclair. That's as bad as Greenwich.

JEBBIE   Don't kid yourself. Greenwich is Gary, Indiana, compared to Upper Montclair. At least you've got some water. The ocean. And the place where the maids live. They had nothing, man. Nothing. No garbage. No grease globs. Nothing. Really nothing.

BOBBY   Upper Montclair.

JEBBIE   I went off for five minutes. That's all it took. Carbon bisulfide. A rag soaked in it over the door. I could smell death. You ever smell death, Bobby?

BOBBY   There isn't one of us alive who hasn't. You know that.

JEBBIE (*Challenges*)   Carbon bisulfide? Your sixty kids? C'mon. (*Remembers*) I tried to move the rag. I went out for five minutes. Five whole minutes. They were gone. I just ran. I ran and ran and ran.

BOBBY   How'd you get up here?

JEBBIE   In a car. I got right into the bastards' car. Rode right into the city with them.

BOBBY   That's beautiful.

JEBBIE   That's how you've got to push, Bobby. That's how you've got to do it. (*Pauses*) But you've done it, haven't you? You made into my place. You're all right. God damned all right. Rats spelled backwards is star!
(*There's a huge, frightening, childlike scream. They both dart downstage left*)

BABY   *WAHHHHHHHHHHHHHH!*

BOBBY   What is it? What is it?

JEBBIE   Easy. Go easy. It's the kid.

BOBBY   I could smell it.

JEBBIE   It's just the kid.
(*A Negro man, wearing diapers, enters, crawling downstage right. He continues to cry and whine, but doesn't see the rats*)

190

BOBBY   He's all black! He's a black baby. My grandfather told me about black babies.

JEBBIE (*Nervously trying to direct the subject away from the* BABY)   I thought he lived in Georgia.

BOBBY (*Moving toward the* BABY)   It's my fantasy. My mother told me. She came up on a train. He told her, but she told me about black babies . . . about my grandfather and the black babies . . . so much that I keep believing he told me.

JEBBIE   (*Calls from the distance*)   What?

BOBBY (*Moves back to* JEBBIE)   I never met my grand-father. I just heard my mother talk about it so much, it's as though I was really there myself. Jesus. Don't let me get you mad. I'm just all excited. A black baby.

JEBBIE (*Playing it down*)   Yeah. So. Big deal. A black baby. We've been living together for so long, I forget he's here.

BOBBY   Can I eat him?

JEBBIE   Huh?

BOBBY   Can I eat him? Bite him? I've never bitten a black baby. I've never bitten anyone. Not in Greenwich. There's nobody. Nobody. You're from Jersey. You know.

JEBBIE   Lay off, kid. Lay back.

BOBBY   What's the matter?
      (*The* BABY *crawls near them, whimpering. They*

191

freeze until the BABY *crawls back to his original spot across the stage from them*)

JEBBIE   Just lay back. Take it easy.

BOBBY   I don't get it.

JEBBIE   Don't try to get it. Just shut up.
(BABY *hears the scuffle and begins to cry again*)

BOBBY   Ughhh. Hey. Hey. Stop it. Ughhh.
(*Gets to his knees. He's shocked. He sees the* BABY *again and goes for him.* JEBBIE *pounces on* BOBBY *again and beats him until he's unconscious.* BABY *is crying now and crawling frantically from corner to corner.* JEBBIE *checks to see that* BOBBY *is unconscious, then crawls to* BABY *and embraces him*)

JEBBIE   Easy, Baby. Easy, boy. It's all right. Don't cry now. Want some milk? Want me to get your bottle? It's in the corner.

BABY (*Talks gibberish babytalk*)   Nooo. Gee gee waa too too meee.

JEBBIE   No milk for my baby? Good baby? (*Cradles the* BABY *in his arms*) Good baby, stop crying. Good baby. That's my baby.

BABY (*Calmed down. Friendly. Recognizes* JEBBIE)   Goo gaa gaa meee? Waa waaa tooo too gee.

JEBBIE   I wish you could talk. I wouldn't let him hurt you. Don't worry.

BOBBY (*Coming to his knees*)   What's going on?

BABY (*Sees* BOBBY *and gets panicky*) *Waa waa dooo mee mee. Gee too tooo baabaa!*
> (JEBBIE *runs to the* BABY *and then back to* BOBBY. *He stares hopelessly at both. His crisis is clear.* BOBBY *is still stunned.* BABY *screams again*)

BABY *Naw naw nee mee gee gee naw naw nooo nooo no no no.*

JEBBIE Please, Baby. Please don't cry. No one's gonna hurt you. Not while I'm here, Baby. I can take care of you. I've taken care of you all this time, right? Don't cry.

BABY *Naw naw naw naw naw naw naw naw naw.*

JEBBIE Don't make that noise. They'll come in again. They come in. Remember when they almost caught us?
> (BABY *crawls around the stage, crying and whining frantically*)

JEBBIE (*Catches* BABY *and cradles him again*) There. Easy. Easy, Baby. C'mon now.

BOBBY Jebbie. What's happening? What's happening? (*Sees* JEBBIE *cradling* BABY) Hey! Hey! What the hell are you doing?

JEBBIE Just shut up, kid. Shut up. You'll make a noise and they'll come. They'll put the rag on you. One sniff and you'll buy it. Shut up.

BOBBY Bite him. Bite him.

JEBBIE They'll put the rag over the door and your kids will be dead. Sixty kids will be dead. You go out for five minutes. All the kids you can make in twelve months will be dead. All your two-month-olds. All your six-month-olds. They'll all be dead. Your wife. Your kids. They'll all be dead. One sniff.

BOBBY   Bite him. Bite his throat.
    (BOBBY *runs for the* BABY, *who is screaming in terror*)

BABY   *Waa waa. Too too mee waa waa. Naw naw naw naw.*
    (BOBBY *pounces on the* BABY *and pins him to the floor.* BOBBY *is just about to bite* BABY's *throat when* JEBBIE *screams*)

JEBBIE   Please. Bobby. Please. I'm begging you. Please don't hurt him.

BOBBY   (*Shocked. Stops*)   Huh?

JEBBIE   Please don't hurt Baby. Don't hurt Baby. Enough babies are hurt. One sniff. Can't you see? Enough babies are hurt.

BOBBY   What's the matter with you?

JEBBIE   I'll let you in. I'll let you in.

BOBBY   What do you mean?

JEBBIE   I'll let you in. Get you the right connections. Give you money. Give you whatever you want. You'll be in. Uptown. Way up here. You'll be in the castle. With me. Stop. I'll let you in. I have kroners. Shillings. Colored

glass. Grease globs. (*Begging now*) Please stop. Just
leave him be.

> (BABY *frantically cries and finally crawls away from*
> BOBBY *to* JEBBIE. BABY *cuddles* JEBBIE's *legs and
> coos*)

BABY *Gaa gaa gee gee gooo.*

BOBBY Oh, boy. I get it. I get it. You're chicken, Jebbie.
You're chicken. That's what they meant. That's what
they meant.

JEBBIE Who?

BOBBY I passed them in the sewers on my way up here.
I walked for days, Jebbie. Days gone. Just to see you.
The famous Jebbie. Jebbie. They told me you were over
the hill, Jebbie. I couldn't believe it. All the stories. Since
I was a kid. The famous Jebbie. What a crock of shit,
huh, Jebbie? Jebbie's a chickenshit from Upper Montclair. That's what it is, right Jebbie? That's the story, the
real story. Jebbie's all over the hill.

JEBBIE I'll let you in, Bobby. Big things can happen.

BOBBY What did you call me? Madras-commuter? Funny,
coming from you, Jebbie. (*Pauses*) Jebbie?

JEBBIE What?

BOBBY (*Simply*) Kill him, Jebbie. Bite him on the neck
on the vein that makes the blood flow like red piss from
an Indian, Jebbie. Find the vein, Jebbie, and eat it up.
Chew Baby's vein, Jebbie. Upper-Montclair-madras-
commuter-family-rat-Jebbie. Chew the vein.

BABY (*Senses the danger. He cries*)   *Naw naw nooo naw naw naw nawwww.*

JEBBIE   Your mother died, Bobby. You smelled death, Bobby. Why more?

BOBBY   Who killed her, you chickenshit bastard? Huh?

JEBBIE   I can let you in. I'll let you in.

BOBBY   Chew the vein, Jebbie. Chew the vein or I'll walk back down the sewers and tell them all, Jebbie. Tell them all so they come up here . . . so they come up where Jebbie's got the best place . . . where Jebbie's on top. Where Jebbie's King. Way uptown where the shit's on the streets and nobody cares but us, Jebbie.

JEBBIE   You'd do that? You'd do that?

BOBBY   You've got a choice, Jebbie. You chew the vein or I chew the vein. Which is it.
      (JEBBIE *pounces on* BOBBY *and grabs* BOBBY's *throat, strangling him with every ounce of strength he can muster.* BOBBY *falls limply.* JEBBIE *breaks* BOBBY's *back over his knee*)

BABY (*Screams and runs about in panic*)   *Naw naw gee sawsss nawww nawww naww nawwwn naawwwnnn nooooo.*

BOBBY (*Struggling hopelessly for his life*)   Don't. Please. Please. Don't, Jebbie. Don't. Take my cheeses. My cheeses. Cheeses.
      (*He's dead*)

BABY (*Crawls about frantically as* JEBBIE *stares at the dead*

BOBBY. JEBBIE *is crying. Suddenly* BABY *stands up and speaks clearly in English*)   Mommy. Daddy. Mommy. Daddy. Rats. Rats. Rats. Help. Rats. Rats. RATS!

JEBBIE   Why? Why? Why? Why?
(*Helplessly to* BABY. *He stares, weeping, as the lights fade. Blackout*)

ABOUT THE AUTHOR / ISRAEL HOROVITZ was born in Wakefield, Massachusetts, in 1939. He was educated in Boston, then studied on a fellowship at the Royal Academy of Dramatic Art in London, from 1961 to 1963. He returned to London in 1965, the first American to be chosen as Playwright-in-Residence with the Royal Shakespeare Company. His first play, *The Comeback,* was produced in Boston when he was seventeen years old.

Mr. Horovitz was awarded a Rockefeller Fellowship in Playwriting in 1968. He won the Vernon Rice-Drama Desk Award for Distinguished Contribution to off-Broadway, the Jersey Journal Best Play Award, and The OBIE Award, all in 1968. His new plays include *Schnozzolla,* produced at the Act IV Theater in Provincetown, Massachusetts, in July, 1968; a new full-length version of *Line,* to be produced on Broadway this fall, and *Chiaroscuro,* a black-power comedy which was produced at the Teatrino delle Sette, Spoleto, Italy, in July, 1968, and directed by the author.

Mr. Horovitz resides in New York City.